How to survive and succeed
as a **SENCo**
in the secondary school

Brian Hepburn

Acknowledgements

Writing this book involved spending longer alone with a computer than is normally considered healthy for anyone over the age of 15. And that excludes the time spent playing Championship Manager and surfing the net for dodgy websites. Apart from the actual writing it meant emailing, talking with and listening to large numbers of people. Some of them made sense and influenced me positively. Some didn't. Some helped just by being there.

My thanks then to all at the organisation formerly known the Learning Support Service; to the SENCos of Walsall, especially Bill Bennett; to Ted Raybould for his work in Chapter 4; and to SENCo Forum, particularly Biff Crabbe for 'How was your day, dear?' Thanks also to many of the staff at St Francis of Assisi RC School, Walsall, who helped either professionally or by letting me play cricket with them, badly.

Last but not least, thanks to my family – Tom and Judith, Mum and Dad – 'I believe in the love that you gave me, I believe in the faith that can save me' (Bruce Springsteen).

Permission to photocopy

This book contains resource sheets which may be reproduced by photocopier or other means for use by the purchaser. This permission is granted on the understanding that these copies will be used within the educational establishment of the purchaser. This book and all its contents remain copyright. Copies may be made without reference to the publisher or the licensing scheme for the making of photocopies operated by the Publishers' Licensing Agency.

The right of Brian Hepburn to be identified as author of this work has been asserted by him in accordance with sections 77 and 78 of the Copyright, Designs and Patents Act 1988.

How to survive and succeed as a SENCo in the secondary school
LL01713
ISBN 1 85503 367 4
© Brian Hepburn
Cover and inside illustration by David Pattison
All rights reserved
First published 2003
Reprinted 2003

Printed in the UK for LDA
Duke Street, Wisbech, Cambs, PE13 2AE UK
3195 Wilson Drive NW, Grand Rapids, MI 49544 USA

Contents

Contents

Introduction

The SENCo in the secondary school faces many challenges. I think the main one is to ensure that students who were not literate when they transferred to secondary school are literate by the time they leave.

There are other challenges, obviously. You have to support students with a dizzying array of medical conditions, disabilities and specific learning difficulties. Part of your role will be to act as medical practitioner – hands up if you've got the job of dishing out the ritalin. The code reminds us, however, that these conditions only count as SEN issues if they impinge significantly on the child's learning. And it's the learning of literacy skills that is our responsibility.

Over 90 per cent of statements are written for general learning difficulties. Putting this into a wider context, the Basic Skills Agency has published research (see Chapter 2, page 24) that reinforces the fact of the link between poor literacy skills and poverty. It seems to me incontrovertible, therefore, that the primary responsibility of a SENCo lies here, in the teaching of literacy skills. No one else in a secondary school has the responsibility or expertise to teach these students to read.

The Code of Practice invests SENCos with the status and offers a structure to enable this to happen. It also spells out the duties of the SENCo, but a lot of those seem designed to take you away from teaching. I think anything that takes the emphasis off the teaching is a mistake and in this book I've tried to show how you can keep your statutory commitments under control so as to be able to carry out your primary function: teaching literacy skills.

This book is not a weighty academic tome – I'd like to think it's the sort of book you could read in bed, highlighter at the ready. I hope it will help you navigate a course to sanity through the reef of madness that is the weight of expectation and workload thrust upon the secondary SENCo today.

Chapter 1
The role of the SENCo

The scene is any corridor in any secondary school in the country. An irate science teacher storms up beside a gloomy-looking SENCo.

Science teacher:	Ah, David, do you have a moment?
SENCo:	Oh, Sue, actually I was hoping to get to the staffroom to pick up a cup of…
ST:	This won't take a minute. It's about Tom Nash in Y7C4.
SENCo:	Oh yes, such a nice…
ST:	The point is, I asked him to make notes on photosynthesis for homework and he handed in a piece of illegible nonsense. And when I asked him to read it to me, he refused.
SENCo:	The poor lad probably…
ST:	Be that as it may, what are you going to do about his writing? I will not accept work of that standard from anybody.
SENCo:	But Tom has not actually been referred to us before. I think he…
ST:	Well, I'm referring him now and I expect to see an immediate improvement. Now you'll have to excuse me, I must get a cup of coffee before my A Level class.
	[Turns and exits]
SENCo:	But…

Enter a geography teacher, sipping from a steaming mug.

Geography teacher:	David, I've been meaning to have a chat with you about Chloe Young in Y9B4. You wouldn't believe how rude she was to me yesterday and it's the same every lesson. I've not had the misfortune of teaching her before and it's come as a bit of shock, I can tell you.
SENCo:	Well, I did mention in the notes to the SEN register I gave you at the beginning of the year…

| GT: | Oh, nobody ever reads that sort of nonsense. Just make sure she behaves better next time I meet her. |

[Exit]

The SENCo gazes longingly at the disappearing coffee, just as…

| History teacher: | David, I'm sorry but I simply have to complain about Jamil Khan's new helper. |

| SENCo: | Teaching assistant. |

| HT: | Whatever… When I asked her to give out the exercise books, she was positively… |

'All teachers are teachers of pupils with special educational needs.'

Whose fault is it that Tom can't write notes, that Chloe always plays up in geography and that Jamil's teaching assistant has an agenda of her own? It's the SENCo's, of course. What's the role of the SENCo? To take the blame for everything. And not only the blame, but also the responsibility for putting it all right. Having made that clear, the rest of this book becomes very straightforward.

Except that, as a result of the 1993 Education Act, the Department for Education and Skills (DfES) produced the Special Educational Needs Code of Practice (1994). A revised version was issued in 2001. This new Code of Practice made one very crucial point: 'All teachers are teachers of pupils with special educational needs.' (Para. 6:2)

Suddenly, it doesn't all rest on the SENCo's shoulders. The SENCo may, of course, get the blame – that's what SENCos do – but other people have to share the responsibility for doing something about it. And if that isn't cause for celebration, I don't know what is.

The Code of Practice

We're now into our second Code of Practice. When it was published, in November 2001, it was reassuringly familiar. There wasn't a lot of difference between the revised code and its predecessor, the 1994 Code of Practice. Paragraph 7 of the Foreword sets out the main changes, which include:

- a stronger right for children with SEN to be educated at a mainstream school;
- new parent-partnership responsibilities for the LEA;
- a new duty for schools to tell parents when they are making special educational provision for their child;
- a new right for schools to request statutory assessment.

Other changes are there to pretend that the SENCo's paperwork will be reduced. You no longer have to keep an SEN register, for example. Well, you may not *have* to, but try running a department without one. On the other hand, there are plenty of things the code says that you *are* expected to do, including:

- attending Year 6 annual reviews;
- reading transfer documentation from the primary school, using it to help 'shape curriculum and pastoral planning for the pupil in the first few months at secondary school' (Para. 6:7);
- distributing this information to other departments and the pastoral team;
- involving the pupil in planning and drawing up targets;
- involving parents.

The DfES realised that most schools saw the original Code of Practice as an obstacle course. You jumped over a series of fences (or stages) until you arrived at the finishing line (or statement). This seemed to go against the spirit of what they had originally intended. In the revised code, levels of intervention replace stages. There is no longer a race for the five hours a week of teaching assistant time. Instead the emphasis is on teaching and learning needs; the problem lies not so much in the child as in the way they are being asked to learn. The SENCo's task has thus become one of identifying appropriate teaching and learning styles, and then persuading other departments to implement them.

"IT'S ALL RIGHT— HE JUST OPENED THE CODE OF PRACTICE AT CHAPTER 6!"

Most secondary SENCos picking up the Code of Practice will have turned straight to Chapter 6: Identification, assessment and provision in the secondary sector. From there they would have turned to the section entitled 'The role of the SENCo in mainstream secondary schools'. This part is detailed and, frankly, scary. There is so much to do!

SENCo tasks

Paragraph 6:35 outlines the job:

- overseeing the day-to-day operation of the school's SEN policy;
- liaising with and advising fellow teachers;
- managing the SEN team of teachers and learning support assistants;
- co-ordinating provision for pupils with SEN;
- overseeing the records on all pupils with SEN;
- liaising with parents of pupils with SEN;
- contributing to the in-service training of staff;
- liaising with external agencies, including the LEA's support and educational psychology services, the Connexions Personal Advisor, health and social services and voluntary bodies.

Paragraph 6:36 breaks this list down into a series of tasks that SENCos are supposed to carry out:

- planning and co-ordination away from the classroom;
- maintaining appropriate individual and whole-school records of pupils at

School Action and School Action Plus and those with statements;

- ◯ teaching pupils with SEN;
- ◯ observing pupils in class without a teaching commitment;
- ◯ managing the effective deployment of other teachers within the SEN team;
- ◯ managing, supporting and training learning support assistants;
- ◯ liaising with departmental and pastoral colleagues;
- ◯ liaising with feeder primary schools;
- ◯ working with the Connexions Personal Advisor in relation to transition planning.

And nowhere in this list does the annual review or the term Individual Education Plan appear. Running annual reviews of statements alone could take as much as half a day a week, on average. And you know how long it takes to write an IEP.

This is scary in the same way that another ride on your favourite roller coaster is scary. You know what's going to come, but when you turn upside down at 250 miles an hour, it's still going to make you scream. When you walk into your office to be met by a desk full of paperwork and a posse of staff and students who all want a piece of you, screaming suddenly doesn't seem such a bad option.

It may be that you are not yet a SENCo, but harbour ambitions to become one. You may be reading this hoping to be reassured that being a SENCo is actually a rewarding, satisfying job. Well, despite the apparently impossible list of demands, I do know SENCos who say exactly that. It is a position from which you can positively influence the lives of youngsters who, without your support, would be left to fend for themselves. You are the person who can enhance their experience of school by pressing for a curriculum that will endeavour to meet their needs, instead of leaving them as mere bystanders in the battle for league table supremacy.

At this point it may be helpful to put all this information together and come up with a job description built around the roles and responsibilities outlined in the code.

How much should you be paid for this? The code says many schools find it effective for the SENCo to be a member of the senior leadership team, and that's the equivalent of 5 points. Many SENCo posts in secondary schools are advertised on 4 points, so that probably puts you on a par with heads of the core subjects. If you're not on 4 points or more, photocopy the pages from the *Times Educational Supplement* that show posts where the responsibility is equivalent to yours, and advertised on 4 points, and politely wave them under your headteacher's nose with an equally polite request for a rise.

'It is a position from which you can positively influence the lives of youngsters who, without your support, would be left to fend for themselves.'

SENCo job description

Job title	Learning support co-ordinator
Points of responsibility	MPS + 4
Line manager	The named person responsible for SEN under the Education Act 1993 (the deputy headteacher)

Role (from SEN Code of Practice, 6:35)

The SENCo is to:

Assume responsibility for day-to-day operation of the SEN policy

- Administrate the learning support department budget efficiently;
- co-ordinate and maintain the learning support base, including purchasing of appropriate resources;
- maintain the SEN register;
- carry out the school's statutory duties for SEN with regard to the Code of Practice.

Liaise with and advise other teachers

- Co-ordinate and contribute to staff INSET on topics relating to SEN;
- participate in pastoral meetings when the SENCo's attendance is relevant and advisable;
- observe other teachers and offer positive, critical feedback on the teaching of SEN pupils, in negotiation with heads of department;
- advise on the purchase or adaptation of materials for pupils with SEN.

Manage the SEN team of teachers and learning support assistants

- Organise timetables for SEN staff;
- co-ordinate and contribute to specialist SEN training;
- co-ordinate and contribute to teaching programmes delivered by learning support assistants (LSAs);
- oversee teaching programmes delivered by teachers.

Co-ordinate provision for pupils with SEN

- co-ordinate and contribute to the teaching of basic literacy skills;
- keep all staff informed of any changes to the SEN register and any relevant developments with pupils already on the register;
- chair the SEN link committee.

Oversee records of all pupils with SEN

- Co-ordinate and contribute to writing and maintaining IEPs;
- be responsible for all records relating to reviews of pupils at School Action Plus (SA+) and those with statements;
- chair and administer annual review meetings;
- co-ordinate reviews for pupils at SA+.

Liaise with parents of pupils with SEN

- Invite parents to review meetings as appropriate;
- address parental concerns on any matters relating to SEN.

Liaise with external agencies

- Invite relevant agencies to review meetings as appropriate;
- act as the first point of contact within school for external agencies on matters relating to SEN.

Non-contact time

We've seen what the code envisages as the SENCo's role. The good news is that it also includes a section entitled 'Time required for SEN co-ordination' that offers the following helpful pointers:

- governing bodies and headteachers will need to give careful thought to the SENCo's timetable in light of the code (6:36);
- access to a telephone and an interview room is desirable (6:36);
- many schools allocate some administrative staff time to help the SENCo (6:36);
- the role is time consuming and therefore it is usually inappropriate for the SENCo to have other school-wide responsibilities (6:37);
- many schools find it effective for the SENCo to be a member of the senior leadership team (6:37);
- many schools have staff, additional to the SENCo, with SEN responsibilities (6:40).

The code, then, sets out what you've got to do and suggests what support you might need from the school to do it. Simple. However, when SENCos gather together in groups of two or more, and when they've finished congratulating themselves on still being sane, talk drifts in the direction of non-contact time. We've got certain responsibilities laid down by the Code of Practice, so how much time do our schools give us to fulfil them?

Is there, in fact, an official level of non-contact time that SENCos can quote at headteachers? Of course not. All you've got is the section in the Code of Practice set out above. It is clear that the code identifies what you need to do, but stops well short of stating how much is enough time to do it. That should come as no great surprise. If the code will not commit itself to identifying achievement criteria with which to place students at each level of intervention, it certainly won't say that you need 53 per cent non-contact time to do the job. So, how do you ensure that you get the time you need?

You might go to your headteacher and complain that other SENCos have less work to do than you but more time to do it in. At this point your headteacher will pat you fondly on the head, ruffle your hair and give you The Budget Speech. The one that goes:

> I'd love to give you a completely blank timetable and I'm sure you would make tremendous use of it. Sadly, there is just no slack in the budget. We need (delete as appropriate) a head of English / three maths specialists / anyone who can hold a recorder to teach music / four dinner staff / a new science block / 120 new computers and my office hasn't been refurbished for over a year. You can see that my hands are tied. How about if I give you an extra 5 per cent credit on your photocopying key?

SENCo time audit

Name: _____

No. of years as a SENCo: _____ No. of points as SENCo postholder: _____

No. of other teachers in department (not from statements budget): _____

No. of teaching assistants in department: _____ No. of students on roll: _____

No of students

at School Action: _____

at School Action Plus: _____

with statements: _____

Task	Time spent (hours per week)
Teaching in a support or collaborative role	
Teaching a subject	
(subjects)	
1 _____	
2 _____	
3 _____	
Administrating annual reviews	
Writing and reviewing IEPs at School Action	
Writing and reviewing IEPs at School Action Plus	
Meeting:	
SEN staff	
Other school staff	
External agencies	
Delivering in-house INSET	
Managing teaching assistants	
Other administrative tasks	
Other tasks (specify)	

Don't misunderstand me. I have nothing against headteachers. They probably would really like to help you and often their hands really are tied by the budget. The only way forward, therefore, is to audit your specific responsibilities against the number of students on the register. For example, you may have 40 students with a statement. Each annual review requires, on average, one hour's preparation, one hour's doing, and one hour's writing up. That's three hours of non-contact time to administer each annual review. There are 40 weeks per academic year, so you require three hours of non-contact time each week, just for reviews. Unless, that is, you're talking about Transition Plan reviews, for which you need at least four hours. The audit form on page 12 could be used to gather the information into a coherent presentation.

If you do this sort of audit, you will have data that you can present as a spreadsheet, a bar graph, or something equally impressive. The interview with your headteacher might then go somewhat differently as you begin with:

> Thank you for seeing me, Ms Simon. I have set up this PowerPoint presentation as a means of facilitating our discussion about the resource implications for my department in the forthcoming financial year. I am currently contracted for 1265 hours a year and, as you can clearly see from the graph on the left...

At this point the headteacher might make an excuse to get rid of you. Headteachers know that 1265 hours has long since been a minimum rather than a maximum number, and even they get embarrassed about this occasionally. However, unless you can actually see the flames spreading, refuse to move. The audit will have thrown up the number of non-contact hours you need. Make your case scientifically and logically, and with any luck you might find yourself with just a little more time in the week.

Annual review

Chapter 9 of the Code of Practice describes how the annual review should be run. The SEN Toolkit, Chapter 9, contains practical support on preparing and running the review.

The LEA will tell you which students need an annual review on a termly basis. In order to prepare the ground, you should seek written advice from:

○ parents;

○ any support service involved;

○ anyone else the headteacher considers appropriate.

Each student's statement will make clear who is involved from the LEA. This written advice should be circulated two weeks before the review meeting. That means you need to ask for advice about six weeks before the review date. Good luck!

You should invite the following people to the meeting:

- the child's parents (or social worker, residential care officer or foster parents for looked-after children);
- relevant teachers (SENCo, head of year, form tutor, relevant subject teachers);
- an LEA representative (the statements officer or admin. case worker, probably);
- an LEA support service representative;
- anyone else that the headteacher considers appropriate.

The final category should certainly include the teaching assistant who works most with the child. However, there may be a payment issue. If the TA is paid only for the five hours they spend with the student, is it reasonable to expect them to turn up in their own time? Not for the TA hourly rate, it isn't. You might be able to arrange the review to coincide with one of the TA's hours with the student. Most annual review meetings take place during the school day, so it should be possible to find a suitable time.

Parents will have access to a parent-partnership officer, employed by the LEA, who can offer objective support.

There is a clear expectation that the child will attend, but ensure you get their views before the meeting. There is nothing more daunting for the child than being asked how they think school is going in front of a roomful of adults, at least some of whom will be relative strangers.

The code suggests that the meeting should focus on the written advice submitted prior to the meeting. More useful is to focus on the targets written in the IEP. In order to do that you will need to have a certain amount of information. The SEN Toolkit suggests it should include the following:

- overall progress;
- progress towards meeting objectives set out in the statement;
- National Curriculum levels (remember NC levels only have to be recorded at the end of each key stage);
- current levels of literacy and numeracy skills.

The SEN Toolkit also advises that you look at:

- continuing difficulties and what strategies have worked;
- significant changes in the student's circumstances;
- changes to their special needs;
- changes to requirements for equipment, aids or access.

There is also a recommended agenda as follows:

① Introductions
② Confirmation of reports
③ Review of progress
④ Recommendations

⑤ Planning for next 12 months
⑥ Other issues
⑦ Date of next review
⑧ Explanation of what happens after review.

It is hard to argue against all this advice from the Toolkit. At the very least it is a protection against criticism of your conduct of the meeting. 'With respect, I was following the DfES guidelines' is enough to deflect most arguments.

Top tips for annual reviews

① Check you've invited everyone to the review (see list above), preferably earlier than the day before.

② Get the child's views before the meeting. A teaching assistant will do the job. Don't put the child through the agony of being grilled in front of a room full of adults.

③ Forget about circulating reports two weeks prior to the meeting. No one ever does, so there's no point in losing sleep over it.

④ Introduce yourself and then everybody else in the meeting. Professionals will be happy to talk about themselves; parents may prefer you to do the talking.

⑤ Focus on the targets in the IEP. Stay away from lengthy discussions about uniform or falling out with friends.

⑥ Let someone else get a word in edgeways. There is a temptation for SENCos to talk too much during reviews. Other people will have something to contribute; otherwise they would not be there. Let them say it.

It is important to have sharpened your ability to chair a meeting. Try to identify beforehand what problems could arise and who will bring them up. If possible, try to diffuse them before the meeting begins. During the meeting, summarise people's points for them if necessary. Don't allow anyone to keep repeating the same point or to introduce red herrings. As you approach the end, don't ask if there is anything else anyone wants to say – unless you are sure no one will! Keep the date of the next review approximate; you don't want people playing with their diaries at this point.

It can sometimes be difficult to bring a meeting to a conclusion, especially if there are contentious issues to be discussed. Everybody will want to have their say, and may not always appreciate when they've finished saying it. Make it clear right at the beginning of the meeting what time you will finish, then when there are ten minutes to go, issue a warning. If all else fails, announce that there is coffee available in the headteacher's office, where they will be pleased to answer any further questions.

SEN policy

Your school will need an SEN policy. Although it would be nice to have an off-the-peg policy, the variety of school situations makes such a thing impossible. What I can offer is a number of headings along with a few hints on what you might include under them. If a policy is to be anything other than a piece of paper that gathers dust in a filing cabinet, it must be a working document, reviewed and updated annually. Therefore it must reflect the working practices in your school. Refer also to the school's equal opportunities and admissions policies.

Exam concessions

One of your more time-consuming tasks will be to organise exam concessions. At Key Stage 4, you do it despite the fact that there will be someone on the staff called the exam secretary, whose job it is to organise exams. But because everyone knows what a good egg the SENCo is, and because the students might suffer if you don't do it, you do it.

There's a continuous flow of questions on SENCo Forum (see page 55) about this subject. Who can have concessions? What will the exam boards require as proof that a student needs concessions? Who is qualified to provide that proof? There is a reference book that contains everything you need to know and, in theory, there will be one in school. It goes under the snappy title *Regulations and Guidance relating to Candidates with Particular Requirements* and is issued by the Joint Council for General Qualifications. This august body comprises the Assessment and Qualifications Alliance, the Edexcel Foundation, the Northern Ireland Council for Curriculum Examinations and Assessment, OCR, and the Welsh Joint Education Committee. If you can't persuade the exam secretary to hand it over, it can be obtained from an awarding body, or downloaded from one of their websites. It's an invaluable resource and ought to sit prominently on your shelves.

The regulations are helpfully designed to run alongside the Code of Practice's four areas of need:

- communication and interaction;
- cognition and learning;
- sensory and/or physical needs;
- behavioural, emotional and social development.

Here is a summary of the important points:

- Just because a student has a statement, it does not automatically follow that they qualify for special arrangements.

SEN policy

Aims of the policy
What do you want the policy to mean to the school? Is it something to do with inclusion, equal rights, curriculum entitlement or commitment to literacy?

Definition of SEN
Copy it out of the Code of Practice (Principles and policies, para.1:3)

Staffing
Describe who, including yourself, comprises the department. If you have anything to show off in terms of qualifications, you could add them.

Resources
Any special facilities or any modified materials for access, for example.

Identification and review
We know that identification is usually easy. But try not to make it look easy. Explain how you go about deciding whether or not a student has SEN. Remember that the code says a child can have SEN at any time, not just on entry.

Register
Who goes on the register and why? And, just as importantly, how do they get off the register?

Complaints
Remember litigation. If parents and children don't feel they've had their concerns dealt with equitably, they may have grounds to sue. Have a clear procedure and follow it, and ensure you can prove you have followed it.

Admission arrangements for students with SEN
Only your responsibility on a technicality, I reckon. This is part of the overall school policy on admissions. Remember that students with statements now get first call on places, and you can't refuse them admission on the grounds that the school can't meet their needs.

Inclusion and National Curriculum entitlement
An interesting test of your philosophy: is it entitlement at all costs, or are you prepared to sacrifice a child's chances in modern foreign languages to ensure they can read?

Partnership and liaison
List the various organisations with whom you liaise. How do you do it?

Review
The policy should be critically reviewed annually, perhaps just prior to the governors' annual report.

- For the vast majority of students, 25 per cent extra time should be enough. This concession does not need permission from the exam board.
- For students with a learning difficulty, evidence of need and a history of provision will be required. The evidence takes the form of a report from either a teacher with appropriate qualifications or an educational psychologist. There is a list appended of all the 'appropriate qualifications'. The list includes mainly those with the words 'specific learning difficulties' or 'dyslexia', so you can guess what's looked for here.
- Readers and amanuenses can be used only with permission from the exam board, using the evidence outlined above.

The problems arise in deciding which students need concessions and whom to turn to if you need a report. In my LEA, for example, there is no support service with the capacity to take on these tasks.

Looking for extra time is the least of your difficulties; if they need it, give it to them. You may, however, have to stand your ground in the face of competing pressures. Parents may feel their offspring will benefit, but you may find no one else agrees. If you do organise extra time, someone is going to have to do extra time on the invigilation front. You can't do it all, therefore you will not be a popular SENCo, but what's new?

The Key Stage 3 SATs are slightly less life and death. But, each year, the boards issue a pamphlet outlining the steps to take in order to gain concessions for students with SEN. The most common concession is extra time, generally 25 per cent, but you may also apply to open papers early in order to make special arrangements such as providing visual aids. You might want to build models of interlocking cuboids for maths, for example. Some students may qualify to use an amanuensis; if so you'll need to brief the TA beforehand, ensuring it is someone who is used to working with that particular student.

It is a good idea to write a desk label for each student who has a concession. As well as giving the student's name, the label should explain what the concession is. It can then be displayed for the benefit of any exam inspector who may drop in.

Money troubles

Have you ever considered how valuable you are to the school? You could save the school a huge amount of money. There have been a few examples already, and more will follow, of former students returning with a lawsuit under one arm, complaining that their needs were not correctly identified or met and your school now owes them several million pounds for ruining their lives, thank you.

We all have nightmares about the child that we really tried to help, but in vain. The one who never turned up for a reading group, or whose parents never answered any of our letters or phone calls. Well, it's OK. All you need are the records that prove you made all those attempts and that the student or parents didn't co-operate. Then be prepared to stick to your guns. However, if you really didn't offer them any help, you'd better be prepared to explain why. There may have been no referrals from other staff, no records from the primary school and no concern raised by the child or their parents. In that case you can argue that you had done nothing because you were never alerted to a problem in the first place. But if you were approached to help and did nothing, you'll have to be able to back up your professional judgement and explain why you did nothing. If you did nothing because there were just too many students and not enough time, that's when the jackpot signs light up and the school pays out big time. That's why you are so valuable to the school. Do your job well and you may save a fortune in litigation costs.

Administrative help

We've looked at what a SENCo's role is, how much you should get paid to do it, and how much non-contact time is needed. But even with a clear understanding of what you're trying to achieve, a pay rise and an empty timetable, there still may not be enough time in the day. There is a move afoot for schools to employ a full-time administrative assistant to carry out all the really exciting jobs like writing letters, keeping the diary, filing and making telephone calls. This is simply invaluable, but there is a catch. Your admin. assistant will set standards of efficiency that you will find intimidating. You may find people ignoring you and going straight to them. If this happens, the reason will be simple, but chilling. They trust the admin. assistant to do things, but not you. At that point, it would be best to wave a white flag, disappear gratefully into a classroom and get back to teaching.

Useful forms

The daily grind of paperwork cannot be avoided, but you can at least make sure that all the paperwork you do meets some need and is of some use to somebody. You can also make sure you have documents that are easy to use and maintain. At the end of this chapter are some forms designed with that in mind, to help with the task of organisation.

You will need to keep records of review meetings at School Action. The IEP review form will help you by keeping the meeting focused on the IEP. The forms entitled 'Monitoring School Action Plus' and 'Monitoring statement provision' help you with precisely those things.

IEP forms can be created using a software package called IEP Writer (see the resources section on page 64 for publisher details). When you use this software to create an IEP, you can pick from a range of pre-written targets for the first five columns and then record your own thoughts for the outcomes in the sixth. There have been some complaints that the targets are not sufficiently specific, but you can add targets of your own to the bank.

IEP review

Student's name: _____ Date of birth: _____

School: _____ Date of review: _____

Targets	Review of targets	Recommendations

Monitoring School Action Plus

Student's name: _____ Date of birth:_____

School:_____

Date	Present	Summary of discussion / action to be taken

Monitoring statement provision

Student's name: _____ Date of birth:_____

School:_____

Date	Target	Progress	Outcome / Comments

Chapter 2
The classroom

Why teach?

In Chapter 1 we looked at the non-contact time SENCos need to discharge their responsibilities in respect of the code. However, the more non-contact time you have, the less time you spend in a classroom teaching. There is a danger that in the panic to ensure that the largely administrative requirements of the code are carried out, the classroom responsibilities of the SENCo are overlooked or, at least, marginalised. One of the SENCos for whom I have the greatest respect argues that the 'SENCoing bit' is the least important part of the job. The SENCoing, he says, is merely the filling in of endless bits of paper, whereas the real job is teaching pupils to read. It's a tough argument to counter.

The code compares the role of the SENCo to that of heads of department, faculty, or year. These people create credibility in the staffroom by their ability to run a department, and through their classroom skills. Can they control a class? Do they teach difficult groups? Do their students get better than expected exam results? Do the students respect them? In other words, regardless of their administrative role, are they good teachers? Peer credibility and respect are as important to the SENCo as to anyone else, perhaps more so. In staffrooms throughout the land, staff do not respect filling in forms as a proper job — especially when those forms require *them* to fill in another form, or several other forms. We know how important marshalling information is for carrying out a successful annual review, for example. The system requires IEPs to have been written, assessments to be carried out and a report submitted by every subject teacher to give an accurate picture of how a student is functioning across the curriculum. The average subject teacher, faced with, say, 40 of these requests a year alongside the mainstream system of reporting to parents, is going to drag their feet, if indeed they get the reports back to the SENCo at all.

I'd argue that the SENCos who have the greatest success in getting teachers to submit the reports are those who attract the greatest respect and credibility in the staffroom. If you want that co-operation, you have to earn it. I think you earn it in the classroom, working with difficult students, and achieving success with them. 'Ah ha,' says Mr Taylor, of the maths department. 'Ms Gardener works miracles with that Year 11 English bottom set. They behave for her; they're mostly going to get a GCSE and a Welsh Board Certificate of Achievement. If she wants me to fill in a form about Carole King in 9ZBH, it's the least I can do! In fact, I'll do it now.'

Whom to teach?

I make it no secret that I believe the number one priority of the SEN department is to teach children to read, write and spell up to a level where they have some chance of succeeding in the wider world. Did you know that 65 per cent of the

'The number one priority of the SEN department is to teach children to read, write and spell'

prison population have such low levels of literacy that they are excluded from 95 per cent of jobs? And that the greatest correlation with exam success is reading age? Statistics such as these convince me that literacy is vital to the life chances of our students. For more about the effects of poor basic skills, see *It Doesn't Get Any Better,* a report published by the Basic Skills Agency (see page 64).

Alongside this, some 90 per cent of statements are written for general learning difficulties, and so it is reasonable to assume that the vast majority of children on your register will be there for that reason. The Literacy Foundation Units are designed to support students at Level 2. The unit on phonics in particular is a valuable resource, although it won't, on its own, be enough. You will need to dig deeper.

Just remember that, developmentally, these students are bottom juniors, if you're lucky. They may not be ready to learn all this academic stuff. You may need to think about a course in reading readiness before you start the literacy teaching.

Teaching reading

There are 1001 ways in which SENCos organise the teaching of reading. In my neck of the woods, Direct Instruction is very popular, being the main recommendation from our educational psychology service. This is a method of teaching, originating in the USA in the 1960s, in which skills such as phonics, sight vocabulary and comprehension are broken down into small steps. Students have to master each step before moving on to the next. The resource used to deliver this is SRA's *Corrective Reading*. It isn't terribly exciting but it seems to be effective and is structured in a way that allows progress to be measured. Also, you don't need to know anything about the teaching of reading to deliver it. Now let's face it, SENCos come from a variety of backgrounds, and not all are trained in the teaching of reading. In a recent survey of teacher training courses, students spent a total of 4 hours, on average, learning about the teaching of reading. Not everybody feels confident in drawing up their own programme. *Corrective Reading* is a handy off-the-peg programme that anybody can teach.

Another approach you could take would be to organise a reading circus in which you set up several reading activities around the room. The students divide up their time between the activities, doing some of each during the course of the lesson. A typical circus lasting an hour might look like this:

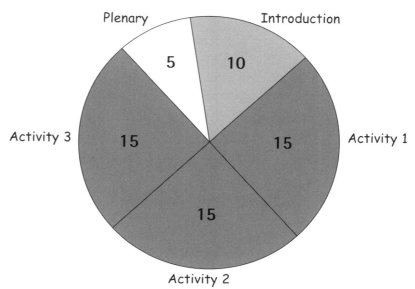

The introduction might be a whole-group mental starter, based on National Numeracy Strategy ideas, or perhaps a drama warm-up such as how many different uses can you make of an everyday object, such as a plant pot? It might be a competitive small-group activity, for example which group can come up with the biggest list of smaller words from a large word? Or it might be a quiet, individual worksheet activity if the class is over lively and needs to calm down. This is also your opportunity to set targets for the lesson or to remind students about targets set previously.

Students then spend the main part of the lesson on the three selected activities. You could try any of the ones suggested in the following list – or whatever you've used that works.

For the last five minutes, get everyone together for a plenary activity. I like the idea of getting together to discuss what you've got out of today's lesson. Professor Tim Brighouse says that the most important question to ask anyone at the end of a day is not 'What have you done today?' but, rather, 'What have you learned today?' At the very least, I'd spend the plenary reading them a story.

Reading circus activities

Reading lab
I'm not a great fan of Reading Labs that used to be a common sight in remedial departments. But I do like *Reading Workshop* from Ward Lock. This box is designed on similar lines to other Reading Labs, but is somehow less of a conveyor-belt experience. (Finish this card and there will another along for you to complete in a moment.) The other advantage is that it's not difficult to set the student at the right level, and progress is easy to monitor.

Silent reading
Assuming you have a comprehensive library of age-appropriate readers, there is no reason why the students should not simply sit with a book that is a

challenging but secure read (not too easy, but not at frustration level). There are a number of publishers that offer audio tapes to accompany their books. A set of Walkmans (Walkmen?) would be a worthwhile investment. You could also organise shared reading or a small group to read a play together. Neither of these is exactly silent, of course, but they do make reading fun.

Recommended reading books

Penguins series, Ginn

- Reading age 7.0 and 8.0
- Cartoon plays for two characters, allowing peer tutoring with readers at different levels

Zoom series, Ginn

- Six sets of books taking children from virtual non-readers to independent readers

Five Minute Thrillers, Ten Minute Thrillers, LDA

- Reading age 8.0
- Just what they say. Finish a complete book in very short space of time.
- Support materials available

Spirals plays, Nelson Thornes

- Reading ages 7.6 and upward
- Genuinely funny and motivating

Headwork Readers, Oxford University Press

- Reading ages 7.0 and upward
- A variety of story types, some more successful than others
- Support materials of high standard

Structured teaching

You could delve back into the National Literacy Strategy for Year 3, or whichever year seems most appropriate, and use learning objectives from there. You could use a Direct Instruction resource such as *Basic Reading for Secondary Students,* which lends itself to teaching in relatively short chunks. Or you could use a programme like *THRASS,* which is becoming increasingly popular in secondary schools.

ICT

Hopefully you are in a room that houses several computers. There are many good software programs you could use; see page 64 for some recommendations. This might also be the time to use an integrated learning package such as SuccessMaker.

Cloze

Practise the use of context clues by playing your own version of Blankety Blank or use a published resource of cloze comprehension exercises.

You might have a range of resources that you have produced yourself, but most departments have a budget for buying materials. Here are a few suggestions of stimulating and interesting fiction that you might want to have on your shelves to support your teaching of reading. No matter what strategy you use to teach reading, students have to see a purpose to it. Enjoying a book sounds as good a purpose as any. These books are all enjoyable.

One SEN teacher I know runs a highly professional publishing activity. The student drafts a story, or writes up some non-fiction research. They then produce a final version on the computer, adding illustrations. The work is printed, laminated and added to the library for all students to read.

'The sentence is the key to being literate'

It is worth mentioning here that the most successful SENCo I know, at least when it comes to teaching reading and then being able to prove his students' progress with data, almost completely ignores reading for the first term with his new Year 7. Everything is done orally. The children are taught how to behave in his room and how to handle sentences. Bill argues that the sentence is the key to being literate: if youngsters can't speak in sentences, what hope have they of learning to read or write in sentences?

Teaching spelling

Again, it's a case of doing what works. I'd want to start by teaching strategies. Just as good readers choose an appropriate strategy to read a 'hard' word, there are different ways to approach spelling. Choice of strategy depends on the word. I'd want my students to be able to handle these for a start:

- Look, Say, Cover, Write, Check
- Mnemonics (e.g. Small Animals In Danger)
- Syllabification (breaking words into syllables – after teaching what a syllable is)
- Exaggerated pronunciation (e.g. Wed/nes/day)
- Use of dictionary
- Personal dictionary
- Spellcheckers
- Electronic spell master
- Flashcards
- Word walls.

Well, perhaps these might not all be classed as strategies, but they are all useful. What more do you want? Then there's all the software you could use (see page 64 for recommendations). I like Wordshark 3. Or rather, my students love Wordshark 3, which is a series of spelling games that use words from carefully structured lists.

Once students know *how* to learn to spell, you can move on to *what* they should learn to spell. Here, the world is your lobster. There are the NLS high and medium frequency word lists, for starters. Then there is a wealth of ideas in the *Literacy Progress Units* for Year 7 that include one called *Spelling Programme*. Whatever else you do, set words to learn for homework regularly, and test even more regularly. Overlearning and mastery are vital for these children.

Teaching writing

Teach writing for a purpose, and drafting, and everybody's happy. If you are leaving a note for yourself on the fridge, you write differently from the way you'd write a letter of application for that SENCo job you're now sure you could do. If you were doing the latter, you would work it up from a few initial thoughts into a series of paragraphs, then after some editing and polishing produce the final version.

I don't understand why more teachers don't flog the concept of drafting. It is true that most of our students hate writing on principle, and drafting means more writing, therefore it is bad. But if they see that the writing has some importance attached to it and that they need to do it as well as they can, they will want to do their best work. Can they produce their best work straight away? No, but they can plan, organise and refine. If they can do this on a computer, where they are not left with a trail of scruffy bits of paper, they will take a pride in it.

The secret ingredient is the sentence. My friend Bill is right. If students can handle sentences, they can organise their writing into whatever form they require to meet the purpose of the task. If the task has no purpose, they may be entitled to ask, 'Why are we doing this?' and they will almost certainly do it badly.

Subject specialism

SENCos are not like heads of subject departments. The head of geography will probably have a geography degree, a PGCE and some years of teaching geography. Their timetable will mostly be made up of teaching geography lessons. SENCos, on the other hand, will also have a degree in a subject and some years of teaching that subject. Their timetable consists of, hopefully, some teaching of reading lessons. Some SENCos get a blank timetable and they can decide themselves how to use the time most effectively. (Be careful on that one, though; see page 23.) However, many SENCos are also asked to teach their specialist subject, often to the bottom set. That way, you solve the school's shortage of subject teachers and you'll still be working with the SEN set.

I'm not a big fan of SENCos teaching the bottom set. It seems to be a good way for departments to avoid responsibility for those students. Ms Gardener can teach Y10ZZ, and we can get on with the important business of GCSE. Even before 'All teachers are teachers of pupils with special educational needs', that seemed wrong. Signing up to teach in a comprehensive school means teaching students of all abilities, regardless of whether they're going to get an A Level in your subject or not.

I don't even think it's good for the SENCo. You may have a managerial responsibility for a particular section of the school population, but you're still a teacher in a comprehensive school. You are therefore entitled to teach across the ability range. Yes, there's a thrill in teaching a 13-year-old to read when everybody else has failed. There's also a thrill in getting a class full of Level 7s and the odd 8, teaching a Year 9 top set English. Bright, motivated kids are a joy to teach. Introduce them to something and they pick it up quickly. Make it interesting and they pick it up and run with it. You just try to channel their enthusiasm. It's great. The downside is that they tend to produce a lot of marking, but if what they've produced is good, even marking doesn't seem so bad.

"AND NOW FOR MORE ON THE FRENCH REVOLUTION IT'S OVER TO Ms WILLIAMS."

Teaching SEN students is a rewarding experience, or it can be. But there's no reason why others shouldn't have a turn with them, leaving you free to be a comprehensive-school teacher, teaching comprehensively.

Collaborative teaching

Not, please note, 'support teaching'. I don't like support teaching. Invariably you're in the classroom to prop up another teacher, who's probably being paid at least as much as you, but who needs you to control their class. No thanks.

Collaborative teaching, however, I usually enjoy. I get equal billing and I get to stand up on my hind legs and perform. And let's face it, this is the reason many of us came into teaching; we're frustrated actors. I also get to plan and review the work. If I'm being particularly generous, I'll even do the marking, which makes me popular with the subject teacher.

The other advantage of collaborative teaching is that there is a reasonable chance the other teacher will pick up something along the way. Often, the main thing they pick up is how many times you go over the same point before you move on. As teachers of SEN students, we know automatically that they won't understand the first time we say something. They either won't have listened or what you've said has been too difficult for them to process. So you say it again, several times, and ask a few pertinent questions. Then you're satisfied that they're ready. The average science teacher will tell them what to do and expect them to get on with it. Of course, if you happen to find yourself in front of a group of top-set students, they will understand first time, even before you've finished waffling. It will be hard to stop yourself from launching into half a dozen different versions of your point. Do try, otherwise you will eventually notice that no one is paying a blind bit of notice, they're too busy getting on with the task in hand. This is always embarrassing.

You may be sceptical about planning the work collaboratively. You may be saying 'When?' The simple answer is that you either find the time or it doesn't get done. In my work in the support service, I have been involved in a number of collaborative teaching projects. Often my involvement came about initially because of a concern about an individual's learning. Usually, however, we quickly agreed that the existing syllabus didn't really meet the needs of many of the students in the group. In some cases, I was then invited to work with that teacher for one lesson a week. The teacher would be given a protected free period and I used my flexible timetable to match their time.

The materials you produce in the course of such teaching will give a clear signal about differentiation. This is an important point, particularly now that it is recognised that 'all teachers are teachers of special needs'. But how do subject staff become teachers of special needs? They have to learn to adapt their teaching styles and their curriculum materials so that they are accessible to students with SEN. What the materials look like will clearly depend on the topic, but a sample of some that came out of one such English department project can be found in Appendix 1 on page 60. It is based on R L Stevenson's *The Strange Case of Dr Jekyll and Mr Hyde* and forms part of a Year 10 unit of work on the pre-twentieth-century novel.

I'm pleased to say that the materials produced for the project were handed on to other teachers in the department and the work we did there is still being used a number of years later. In an ideal world, we would have had meetings for those teachers to give feedback and then we would have modified the unit in the light of the criticism. Sadly, even in the world of a support service, there are limits to the amount of time that can be invested. And that's why the materials are still being used, rather than revised and improved.

How do you organise this sort of work? It depends on how much you and the heads of departments trust each other, and whether you're happy to accept the blame if anything goes wrong. If you are unhappy about either of those points, I would recommend a written agreement. This way, both parties know where they stand. Agree on what you expect from each other, and write it down. You could use a form along the lines of the one that follows.

The possibilities are endless. Just don't lose sight of the fact that, first and foremost, you are a teacher. You can worry about the forms later.

Learning support department

Subject agreement

Teachers involved: _____

_____

_____

When? _____

Where? _____

Students involved?　　Y/N　　If so, who? _____

_____

_____

Project duration: _____

Outcome: _____

_____

_____

_____

Signed:

_____　SENCo

_____　Head of department

Date: _____

Chapter 3
The department

In your role as a SENCo you need structured support. This is provided by your department, but it's up to you to set it up in a way that supports you effectively. There are a lot of things to think about.

Name

What is your department called? Are you Learning Support? Special Needs? Individual Learning? Pupil Support? Something Else? So long as you're not still the Remedial Department, it probably doesn't matter. What is wrong with Remedial Department? It was a reflection of the medical model that suggested the student had something wrong with them, like measles. The 'remedial' bit suggested that the teacher would cure them of their educational ills. Pupil Support was better, but still seemed to suggest that the problem was only within the child. Whilst it may be true that the child needs support, that may not tell the whole story. (We'll come back to this when we look at what everyone else can do to help.) In these enlightened days of inclusion we recognise that there is a chance the problem lies outside the student, perhaps within the curriculum or in a mismatch between teaching and learning styles. If that is the case, then Learning Support seems to fit best.

Office

You have to have an office of your own. Who else on the staff has an office? All the important people: the headteacher, the deputies, the members of the leadership group, the caretaker…

Your role requires you to exercise a degree of confidentiality equal to that required of a head of year. You are going to need to talk to parents, children and outside agencies about stuff that no one else should hear. You need to build trust and respect; try doing that with the PE department throwing sandwiches at each other across the room. End of story.

You will also need somewhere to house the paper equivalent of plankton. In terms of equipment, a fleet of filing cabinets is your first priority. You are going to have so many bits of paper to process that if you can't tuck them away tidily, the only solution will be to eat them. If you do that you'll only have to write them out again, so filing cabinets are favourite.

There is then all the fun of deciding how to organise them. You could file by School Action, School Action Plus and statement. (Except, do you need to keep records on the SA students? Maybe, maybe not.) Or you could do it by year group. Or by type of learning difficulty. Or by shoe size…

Another essential item is the biggest desk you can fit in; you'll need the space to balance as much as possible in front of you, as well as providing the largest possible barrier between you and unwelcome visitors. You should also treat yourself to the most expensive chair the school will buy for you. You are going to spend a lot of time in it; you might as well be comfortable.

Don't underestimate the value of a kettle and a jar of coffee, and some biscuits. A fridge is optional. On one level, it's fairly obvious why you want to provide some basic refreshments, but there is a serious issue lurking here. What sort of image do you want to promote? Do you want to run the sort of department where staff and students feel encouraged to drop in at any time to discuss their latest crisis? In that case you can afford to have the office looking a little dishevelled and homely. Your guests will perch on top of a few half-written IEPs and the last three weeks' job sections from the *TES*, and find it all quite comforting. Your open-all-hours philosophy will probably make you popular and successful. Solving people's problems is almost a requisite of the job — and a happy workforce is a productive workforce.

Unfortunately, there is a negative correlation between success and survival here. If you are always available to other people, you will have no time for yourself. Eventually, you will crack up. Therefore, you will need to spend some quality time with yourself, getting on with some work or even just chilling. One way to achieve this, of course, is to keep your office scrupulously clean and tidy, with everything corralled into filing cabinets or box folders or, preferably, shredded. This strategy will ensure that visitors will be too intimated by the clinical atmosphere to stay. They will leave quickly, in case they make the place untidy.

The telephone

When you've spent most of your day on the phone with parents, social workers, nurses, parents, educational psychologists, LEA officials and parents, you'll be daydreaming of exactly what you'd like to do to Alexander Graham Bell with the blunt end of the receiver. Sadly, you can't live without a phone. All those people and more are going to want to ring you to make sure you sort out some emergency or other that has just befallen a child or, more importantly in some people's eyes, some piece of paper. You are also going to need to contact them at some point with a genuine problem affecting the life of one of your staff or students.

Shelves

Now you've got your own office, clearly you want it to look impressive. One way of doing that is to have an imposing collection of literature on your shelves. You'll certainly need copies of the following:

- *Special Educational Needs Code of Practice*
- *SEN Toolkit*

◐ *National Curriculum 2000 Inclusion Statement*
◐ *National Standards for Special Educational Needs Co-ordinators* (TTA)
◐ *National Special Educational Needs Specialist Standards* (TTA)

It helps to find out what resources you can get free. The DfES is a good source of vital documents, as is the Basic Skills Agency. I'm a big fan of the BSA. Make sure you have their most recent catalogue and check out their website as often as you can. They do produce teaching materials, but their main strength is in the research department; their reports and videos are invaluable. Also, if your LEA has any useful documents such as SEN policy or a set of criteria for assessment or acceptance by a support service, keep them handy. They are good to have around to thrust under the nose of an LEA officer.

ICT

A computer is surely now essential for the job. The SEN register needs to be maintained electronically, you need access to the school record system, you will probably want to turn out forms (such as those offered in Chapter 1), letters and worksheets – the list is endless. You should not have to go and beg access to someone else's computer. Ideally, your computer will be connected to the school network. It will also have access to the Internet and you should be able to email from your own desk.

Access to the Internet also opens up another source of invaluable support. SENCo Forum is an online newsgroup primarily for SENCos. This is simply a group of people who keep in regular contact with each other, providing an invaluable colleague support system. For more on this, see Chapter 6 (page 55).

'There is no point in putting a student on the register if you don't have time to do anything about them.'

The SEN register

At the heart of a department's organisation is the SEN register. Ensure that it is legal. Have you informed parents and got their consent? Physically, it ought to be kept on a spreadsheet, probably divided up into School Action, School Action Plus and statements, with each section arranged by year. If you're particularly organised, you could add further details such as the reasons for being on the register, medical history and names of external agencies involved in each case.

But, who goes where? Much of the groundwork should have been put in before transfer from the primary school. You will build links with primary SENCos, ensuring that they inform you of children on their registers. Pastoral liaison between schools may fill in a few blanks. A scrutiny of Key Stage 2 SAT scores will provide further information. Within the first few weeks of term, subject teachers will let you know about any student you might have missed.

The real issue about the register is whether you have the resources to do something about all the students on it. There is no point in putting a student on the register if you don't have the time to do anything about them. I know schools that have over 50 per cent of the students on the SEN register. That being so, the remaining minority might be the ones whose educational needs are not being met – it might be better to put them on the register instead! At least you'd have a chance of seeing them from time to time. The point, I would argue, is that the register cannot be a criteria-referenced tool. You know which children need help, but if you've got 100 students coming into Year 7 with reading ages less than 9.06, you cannot work with them all. You have to put on the register only the ones you can teach. The rest will have to be supported by the school's literacy policy, the Literacy Progress Units and the Key Stage 3 National Literacy Strategy.

You should also consider how children get off the register. What do they have to achieve to be removed from it? It might be something to do with achieving independent levels of literacy, or it might be when a barrier to learning has been overcome. You ought to know what it will be for every student you put on the register. Some of them will be 'lifers', but a good number should escape, if your teaching is successful.

If a student does enough to be removed from the register, or even to be moved down a level, it should be cause for celebration. Make a fuss; throw a party; issue a certificate. This ought to be seen as a real achievement in the student's life. Don't acknowledge it apologetically or let it slide by unnoticed. It may not quite be a whole-school assembly deal, but it ought to be marked.

> 'If a student does enough to be removed from the register ... it should be cause for a celebration.'

Who goes where?

So, how do you decide which students should be at which level of intervention? It is easiest to start at School Action and work up.

School Action

The first question is who should be on the register in the first place. The majority of pupils in a comprehensive school will have their needs met through a differentiated curriculum – or they will if there is such a thing. If subject teachers provide work at the appropriate level for the students in front of them, regardless of whether it's a mixed ability or setted group, most children will not have learning difficulties. This is essentially what the code says, and I wholeheartedly agree. Whether all subject teachers will do this effectively is another matter, and one that is addressed in Chapter 4.

There will be a significant number of students who transfer to you with literacy and/or numeracy skills below a functional level. You will have to teach them in order to get them as close to that level as possible. They should all be at School Action with group educational plans (GEPs), which should be reviewed two or three times a year. Twice, if everything is fine. You'll be working with them in groups, teaching to common targets.

School Action Plus

It isn't difficult to spot which students fail to make progress in reading groups. They will be the ones you consider moving to School Action Plus. Paragraph 6:64 of the Code of Practice details triggers for SA+ and explains the placement of students with behavioural, sensory, physical and communication needs. (Literacy and numeracy problems are easier to categorise and place.) Also, if there is an external agency involved and the student does not have a statement, then they will automatically be at SA+. These students will need IEPs.

Statements

Paragraph 6:70 says that very few students will need to go on to formal assessment, and that the decision to refer is grounded in the lack of progress made at SA+. The code describes your register as a pyramid, with numbers of students decreasing as you move up the levels. The reality is likely to be more of an hourglass, reflecting the fact that, as a SENCo, you will want to attract the extra funding that a statement brings; LEAs have little to offer in terms of support at SA+. For many students there is, therefore, little point in keeping them at SA+. If they are not going to end up being referred for formal assessment, they can be put back to SA.

Screening

Screening has become a wonderful euphemism. We actually mean testing, but are too polite to say so. And it really is testing. What's the greatest blight on a teacher's life these days? Apart from missing out on a social life, that is. Paperwork. So what's the first thing we do when we get new students into Year 7? We give them copious tests: reading, spelling, verbal, non-verbal, CAT, MIDYS, YELLIS…All of which create more paperwork.

I know of Year 6 children who have gone to the secondary school on a 'fun' induction day, only to be frogmarched into the hall, where pens have been thrust into their hands and assessments begun. How traumatising must that be? Alternatively, you could launch some sneak raids behind enemy lines. I know of at least one school that sends a platoon of TAs to carry out reading and spelling tests, and I'm not convinced of the wisdom of this. TAs are supposed to be on the students' side when they need help in school. I think if you use them for testing, you risk establishing a climate of fear and mistrust even before the school year begins.

But why does a SENCo need to test? The CAT, SCAT and BRAT tests are probably beyond your control and they may even help with year-wide target setting. But you'll know who has a statement or is at SA+, because you went to the Year 6 review. (Or reviews. The code says LEAs have to offer places to students with statements by January of Year 6. The annual review will have to be held early in the autumn term. You'll be invited to that, but it's much too early to make decisions about Year 7. So you may find you need another review in the summer term, thereby doubling the number of reviews you need to attend.)

I'm not against assessment *per se*. However, a test is only as good as the action that follows it. If there is no action and the results sit in a filing cabinet, 'just in case', the test was useless. Now there are varying degrees of sitting in a cabinet.

The shape of the SEN register, according to the Code of Practice

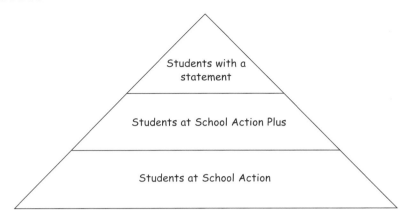

The reality of the shape of the SEN register

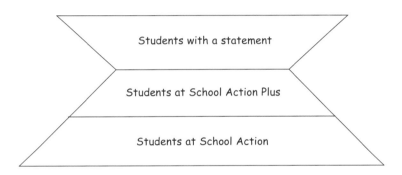

Sometimes results are taken out, dusted down and compared with the previous year's score. I'm not even a big fan of that. On the other hand, I am in favour of the system used by my colleague Bill, who will flash reading test scores at people at the drop of a hat. The tests are given on the pretext of providing a placement on a reading programme. Actually, they don't. All the students who need help with reading are bunged together and given help. But the testing does tell Bill when it's time to stop and the test results provide him with the evidence he needs to demonstrate that what he does works. He can show the headteacher and senior management that he is making their life easier; if he teaches a student to read, the student will get better exam results – and schools live and die by exam results. The headteacher is grateful to Bill and Bill gets what he wants – to be empowered to help the students who need it. So, testing can be A Good Thing.

Even so, I'm not convinced you really need an initial test for the whole of Year 7. When the students come into Year 7, you know the ones who can't read. Or you soon will when their teachers grab you in the corridor. Test them quickly (with something like the NFER Group Reading Test) – 25 minutes out of these students' lives is an investment rather than a withdrawal. After that, get working with them. Build up some trust and confidence. Then you can test to confirm that they're making progress. You'll know whether they're improving as readers and at that point the test is guaranteed to provide good news for the student, the parents and you. Everybody wins.

OFSTED

The classic OFSTED SEN story comes out of a meeting of secondary SENCos. Several of the schools represented had just been inspected and a question arose about withdrawing children. One SENCo said that her inspector had criticised her for running a withdrawal system. And, yes, you've guessed, another SENCo said he had been criticised for *not* running a withdrawal system.

Whatever the rights and wrongs of this, the point is an important one: what you actually do doesn't matter, but it has to be good and you have to be able to prove it's good. What does matter is that you have records that show you do the statutory stuff formally. Will they find evidence of annual reviews being carried out appropriately? Will they find IEPs written and kept up to date, and even being used? Will they find evidence of progress? If, like Bill, you can pull out data that demonstrate that by the end of Year 8 almost all children are independent or functional readers, you have succeeded. Everything else you can argue about.

And you should argue. If you're doing something that OFSTED doesn't like, but you know works and can prove works, they will have to back down. If they don't, you have a legitimate grievance. If you're doing something that you can't prove works, and OFSTED jumps on you, you're on your own.

Now what?

You've assembled a team of colleagues and a well-stocked office, so how is your department going to operate? I like the idea of a department that regularly has children around. The busier you are with them, the less time you have to spend worrying about paperwork and other adults. You might consider having a lunchtime drop-in surgery with informal learning activities. I spent a happy lunch hour at a school in Birmingham with this kind of arrangement. There was a small group in one corner playing Scrabble, a couple of sixth-formers listening to several younger students reading, a cluster of children busy on a computer with SuccessMaker, and a Year 8 girl sitting with headphones on, listening to an audio tape and following the story in a book. The main point here is that your job is to set it up; you don't need to be there on a regular basis. Leave that to TAs, sixth-formers, or parent volunteers.

Your department's ticking away, children are being taught to read. How are you going to spend your day? I asked one secondary SENCo how he got through the school day. His senior management team had asked him a similar question, so he wrote the piece on pages 61–3. I thought it was a terribly sad existence, full of trivia and things beyond his control, or things that ought to have been someone else's responsibility. He was a little shocked, saying that it wasn't that bad really. I'll leave you to judge.

Chapter 4
Interdepartmental liaison

The first question to ask about your links with subject departments is what do they want from you? However, this is such a dangerous question that on no account should you ever utter it aloud. The answer would be 'everything', and you can't provide everything. The fictitious dialogue at the beginning of Chapter 1 (pages 6–7) highlights an important truth: subject teachers do blame the SENCo if students can't read *Spotlight Science* or *Arc en Ciel*. They blame you too when students can't write in sentences or spell their own names accurately. So you need to set up literacy groups to teach them these skills. Now you just need to work out from which subjects to withdraw them.

Supporting students

At this point you need to be very clear about why you are offering a student support. For example, is Ben naughty – sorry, does he have behavioural needs because he has low levels of basic skills and is trying to avoid doing work he knows is beyond him? Or is he a boy who has never learned the importance of sitting still and concentrating, and who will probably cope with work in the mainstream classroom if he has a little help to keep on task and is provided with a little extra explanation? If he has low levels of basic skills, then I suggest he ought to be withdrawn and put on a programme of basic skills teaching that will enable him to get as close to functional levels of literacy as he can manage. (By functional levels, I mean reading and spelling ages of 9.06 years.) If, however, Ben already reads at 9.0 years but is struggling in lessons, I would deploy support in the classroom. See Chapter 5 for more on classroom support.

So, your next challenge is to find lessons on the timetable from which to withdraw Ben. Then you'll have to chat to the relevant head of department. Of course, you are trying to strike the best deal for Ben and, in the long run, the department. The better Ben reads, the better his exam result will be. But every head of department says you can't possibly take Ben out of their lesson. He'll fall behind and never catch up. Ben is entitled to a broad and balanced curriculum, you know. He'll miss quadratic equations, or irregular French verbs, or land use in the Kalahari Desert. Sorry, you'll have to ask someone else.

How can you teach Ben the literacy skills everyone knows he needs if you don't have any time? Of course, you could easily take him out of assembly or PHSE or PE or other things that don't matter. So, the Kalahari Desert matters, but learning to avoid getting pregnant, or finding out about the next football practice, or participating in the form's play in front of the rest of the year don't? What are Ben's priorities? How can you ensure that Ben gets what he needs?

This is where status and pay are all important. If you are an important enough member of the hierarchy, you just decide for yourself when you want to teach the students, draw up the timetable and begin teaching. If you are very unlucky, there will be a truculent head of modern foreign languages who will come gunning for you, demanding that all the young people are returned to their Spanish lessons immediately. Don't get involved in the argument; just say no. Of course, saying no doesn't always come naturally. In their admirable desire to effect as much positive change in their students' lives as possible, SENCos tend to say yes to most things. 'Yes, I will join the working party on Teaching and Learning Styles'; 'Yes, I will organise the exam concessions for the Key Stage 3 SATs'; 'Yes, I will take the Year 8 football team that no one else likes.' But life is too short to get involved in arguments that you can't win. The head of modern foreign languages knows that once students start being withdrawn and actually learning something somewhere else, everyone will realise that they could be doing something useful with the time they currently spend gazing blankly at a teacher who is trying to tell them something, the meaning of which completely escapes them. If only she would speak in English!

Some SENCos try to accommodate other departments by having floating timetables. Every half-term or so, the students start missing lessons in a different subject. This seems to me to miss the point completely. This sort of rolling programme simply maximises the disruption to student and department. The poor subject teacher is never sure who is there, or for how long or how much they have missed.

Another system used in some schools is to have students withdrawn from the first, last or middle 20 minutes of a lesson, on the grounds that they won't be missing much and can catch up in the lesson. This is a recipe for disruption on the scale of a fire alarm going off three times a lesson. You simply have streams of students wandering the school, creating chaos and interrupting lessons willy-nilly.

'You'll return the students as more effective learners.'

This is not a situation that can be resolved in a pain-free manner. The students have to come out of someone's lesson. Tell everyone where the time will be taken and let them cope with it. You'll return the students as more effective learners. You *will* return them as more effective learners. If you don't teach them to improve their literacy skills, you will be sunk, regardless of how important you are.

Supporting teachers

Apart from teaching them to read, is there anything else departments want from you? Well, they'd probably also like it if you could support them while they try to teach feudal England, or osmosis, or matrices. What subject teachers actually want is someone to take the discipline problems from them, or to make sure Yasmin at the back copies the work down accurately with the title underlined using a ruler.

I don't believe that support work is part of the SENCo's role, although by all means you can give advice on strategies. If Yasmin can't copy accurately, don't make her copy. She won't be able to read it back later anyway, so what's the point? If the teacher really needs someone else to ensure that she understands the task, then maybe they need to reassess their teaching methods — and you can offer strategies on that, too. Perhaps Yasmin has a statement and has five hours of TA time. You might consider putting the TA into that lesson. But you need to know how the teacher intends to use them effectively. Sitting next to Yasmin, reminding her to write on the lines, isn't a good use of time for a TA, and there's no chance of having one just for that.

What you could offer is a term's collaborative teaching, where you and the subject teacher jointly plan and deliver a scheme of work in such a way that Yasmin and all the other Yasmins stand a fighting chance of learning something positive. And when you've finished, the department has got something tried and tested that can be used again when you've gone to help someone else. (See Collaborative teaching, page 29.)

Supporting students with emotional and behavioural needs

So far in this chapter, the discussion has related to students who have general learning difficulties. Equally, if not more, important are those with emotional and behavioural difficulties. Heads of department will want to know what you are going to do about James, who keeps disrupting the lesson. They've been to see the head of year and nothing's been done. Now it's up to you. I think you really do have the short straw here.

First, you have to ask whether James really does have needs in the area of behavioural, emotional and social development, as described by the code, or is he just unruly? The distinction is vital. He should be included on the register if his behavioural needs lead to his having learning difficulties, whereas the unruly youth in middle-band class is not your responsibility. But, if he is on the register, the school cannot now exclude him for behaviour that is described by his need. In other words, if he is on the register because he has Tourette Syndrome and swears constantly, the school can't take offence and exclude him because he swears at a lunchtime supervisor.

But let's say that James has been accurately placed on the register. You are his first line of support in the school. You've probably set up a system so he can come and find you when things get too much for him. Your job is to find time to sit down with him and review what happened in the lesson, and talk about his targets and how he is trying to meet them; in short, the whole counselling bit.

Subject-specific IEPs

We've seen that subject teachers have a responsibility to plan and deliver strategies to support students at School Action. Your job as SENCo is to 'co-ordinate the planning of the pupil's IEP' (Para. 6:55), in other words write it. You are, of course, supposed to involve other staff, but this might be easier said than done.

Nevertheless, even at School Action Plus, delivery of the IEP 'will be the responsibility of subject teachers' (Para. 6:67) and I believe that by the time you get to children on statements, there is a burden of responsibility on teachers to contribute actively. They have a statutory responsibility to contribute to IEPs and to annual reviews. As SENCo you have a responsibility to produce an IEP for the student. This will deal with overall targets connected with the student's needs. The history department may not want to know how you intend to teach the student to read, but it ought to know that they need to learn to read and state how it will help support the process. We know how difficult it is. Is there a system we could set up that will be of use to the student and the teacher, fit in with existing departmental policies and require the minimum of extra work?

The solution I propose involves the use of subject-specific IEPs and is based on a system developed by a secondary school in Walsall.

The work was instigated after an OFSTED report said the school's SEN department was fine but they weren't happy with the contribution being made by subject staff. As you can imagine, OFSTED's word carried some weight, certainly more than that of the SENCo, who had been saying much the same thing and being roundly ignored.

A group of departmental SEN reps discussed how they might beef up their contribution, and in particular how a subject-specific IEP might look, if it were to be workable and even useful. At best this seemed an unlikely prospect: the chances of being able to impose a structure which generated bits of paper that sat in filing cabinets all year were low. If, on the other hand, a system could be developed that fed into existing departmental assessment policies and was seen to benefit staff and students, the chances just might be improved. Thus they developed a system of subject-specific IEPs that works as follows.

Each subject department generates a bank of targets, for example the maths department came up with these:

- to recognise an agreed percentage of mathematics words from the Year 7/8/9 list as set out in the Key Stage 3 Numeracy Strand;
- to improve mental arithmetic skills;
- to learn 1–12 multiplication tables;
- to regain confidence in their own work and in their ability to make progress in mathematics;
- to improve their aural skills in mathematics;
- to increase their participation in mathematics activities through, for example, oral and group work;
- to use mathematical equipment correctly;
- to learn the whole-number complements to 10, 20 or 100;
- to make effective use of ICT equipment, such as calculators;
- to produce accurate diagrams, charts and graphs.

The areas of concern for each student are recorded by the SENCo, generated from the overall IEP and from the statement, in the 'key areas of communication, literacy, mathematics, and behaviour and social skills to meet the pupil's needs' (Para. 6:59). Each subject department then uses these as a basis for choosing three targets from their department's bank. These targets are added to subject IEP forms, like the one on page 44, and posted on shared areas on the school computer network. The whole process, therefore, can be set up electronically. The SEN department, through a mail merge system, provides the information about each student at the top of the form. The only work required of departments at this point is to indicate which three targets have been chosen for each student. As the year goes by, a strategy for meeting the targets is planned (or employed, depending on whether you like to be ahead of or behind yourself) and recorded on the IEP.

When annual reviews come round, a decision is made about whether the targets have been met, and boxes are ticked. The evidence to justify decisions comes from whatever assessment criterion the department was using as it went along. Often that could take the form of a portfolio of work; the student will have been involved in monitoring their targets throughout the year, deciding which piece of work meets which target, and keeping a photocopy of the work. That work is the evidence for the decision about whether the target is met.

The subject IEP form is then printed out and some additional information noted (using a form such as the one on page 45). The form is returned to the SENCo and used in the annual review. The subject teacher may be able to attend the review, but failing that the subject IEP form provides their input in an accurate and focused manner.

Workable? You bet. This kills several birds with one stone. It fulfils statutory obligations, it's useful for subject teachers, it's easy to carry out and it takes up little time. Moreover, the students think it's fun and it's an easy way into the pupil's views part of the code. How many different ways have you tried to get Lee to tell you more than he's 'doing all right'? In fact, Lee has been working on these targets for the best part of a year, is probably proud of his achievements and really wants to talk about them. Here you have a structure for discussion.

Supporting language needs

Hands up if you've ever worried about whether one of your students is actually learning something in, say, history. As my colleague Bill says, how can they cope with Henry II when they don't understand last Tuesday? The answer is that they don't. They don't understand last Tuesday because they haven't learned a variety of concepts concerning time. Therefore, they have no hope of comprehending feudal England.

Then there is the issue of language skills. If you have a group of students in a mainstream classroom who score percentile rank 5 or lower on a test of receptive language, they are not going to understand the majority of what the average

Subject IEP

Subject: _____

Student's name: _____ IEP date: ____/____/_____

Year group: _____ Teaching set: _____ Code of Practice stage: _____

Requirements for special educational provision
Small group work ☐   In-class support ☐   Other ☐

Target:			
Strategies used	Target achieved		
	Yes	Part	No
Evidence	☐	☐	☐

Target:			
Strategies used	Target achieved		
	Yes	Part	No
Evidence	☐	☐	☐

Target:			
Strategies used	Target achieved		
	Yes	Part	No
Evidence	☐	☐	☐

Staff involved			
Review date			
Evidence attached	Yes ☐		No ☐
I / We wish to attend the review meeting	Yes ☐		No ☐
National Curriculum level		Key stage	Level

Signed _____ Date _____

Subject IEP

General information for review

Subject	Cause for concern? Y/N	Details
Behaviour and attitude		
Homework		
Understanding of concepts		
Task completion		

Classroom support Y/N	Details
Please comment on the effectiveness of the support received.	
Are there any changes to the nature of the provision needed?	
Any other comments?	

geography teacher has to say about volcanoes. Then there is all the incidental stuff that the teacher will say. Much of this is couched in terms that the student with poor receptive vocabulary scores will simply not be able to fathom.

I'm indebted to the staff at one of the secondary schools I visit for inviting me to help to look at this precise problem. They had a group of Year 7 students who shared an inability to understand a word that the teacher said. As the year went on, their behaviour steadily grew worse. Some dedicated and concerned teachers had tried an assortment of teaching and classroom management strategies but to no avail. The general consensus was that these students signalled a real difficulty in the Key Stage 3 curriculum. The National Curriculum tells these teachers what they should teach, but the children did not have the language or the concepts to be able to cope with it.

The school set up an 'alternative curriculum' for this group when they got into Year 8. Departmental staff would still teach them, but they would have an extra teacher, albeit with unqualified status, as well as access to TAs. The two unqualified staff would be with the group for all but the practical lessons. The teaching staff would be encouraged to look at other key stages for the curriculum content.

Staff would not be thrown in blind. The school's educational psychologist organised several assessments with direct teaching implications. These included the following:

- Some simple problems to treat the students' understanding of temporal instructions. For example, cards with pictures together with instructions such as:

  BEFORE you point to the scissors, point to the keys;

  INSTEAD OF pointing to the pen, point to the boy.

- A test for basic concepts, with questions such as:

  Which dog is NEAREST the stairs?

  Which tree is the SMALLEST?

- The use of the British Picture Vocabulary Scales test, in order to measure receptive language. This was used by TAs who were first trained by educational psychologists. The TAs were also asked to record any instructions that teachers gave the group. They came up with a list that included:

  Write a paragraph and fill in the gaps using the key words from the textbook.

Make notes in the back of your exercise book.

Anyone confused?

I'll tell you what you need to do in a moment.

The purpose of collecting these examples was not to have a laugh at the teacher's expense. (Although 'Some people are developing attitudes' is rather amusing.) Rather, it was designed to show teachers the complexity of the instructions they were giving these students, particularly when their receptive language scores are taken into account.

There is now a bank of data, test scores and lesson observations that help to provide a picture of the barriers to learning that need to be overcome. Few of the gaps in the students' skills or knowledge would be filled by the mainstream curriculum. With an idea of their actual attainment, backed up with an understanding of how teachers' language can make matters worse and a willingness to look beyond the Key Stage 3 curriculum, this school is beginning to provide a pathway to success.

Chapter 5
Teaching assistants

Your department will have some teaching assistants, or do you call them something else? learning support assistants? ancillaries? classroom assistants? The possibilities are endless. The DfES preferred term is teaching assistant (TA), and I'm more than happy to go along with that.

Except that, as we know, language is everything and the term teaching assistant hasn't come about by accident. Already, the Literacy Progress Units are designed to be taught by TAs. They've come a long way from being the people who washed out the paint pots for early years teachers. Unless you count pay and conditions, that is. We are increasingly asking TAs to carry out a teaching role.

How many of them do you have? Numbers seem to range from 8 to 21, which suggests that there are likely to be a lot of bodies looking to you for leadership. To whom do they belong? The basis on which TAs are employed makes a difference to all concerned. TAs may be paid from a centrally funded statements budget. In that case, there are probably strings attached, like having to work with statemented children. A TA funded in this way will spend almost all their time with the statemented individual, and quite rightly, too. On the other hand, TAs funded directly by the school budget come with enormous flexibility – but your school budget probably won't run to many of them.

Another possible scenario is where LEAs have delegated the statements budget directly to schools. The formula tends to be based on overall numbers rather than on individual cases. That way the school gets the best of both worlds. It has extra funding which is earmarked for the SEN students. Therefore the TA can perform the flexible role, with an emphasis on the individual, but by no means to the exclusion of other tasks. Indeed there are LEAs where funding has been devolved for students at School Action and School Action Plus.

The system works only if the money is ringfenced and closely monitored by the LEA. Experience suggests that the money often disappears into the school budget for general use and the LEA, underfunded and undervalued, cannot keep a close enough watch on behalf of the students.

TA research

Here in Walsall I have spent an increasing amount of time with TAs, delivering training, monitoring work with statemented students, and trying to solve disputes between TAs and SENCos. I have also been involved in small-scale research projects, looking at how TAs work. Much of the rest of this chapter draws on the findings of that research.

Main findings of the TA research

◐ TAs often have a more detailed knowledge of a student than anyone else in a secondary school.

◐ The most effective relationships between TAs and students are formed on the basis of mutual respect.

◐ TAs have a student's perspective of a lesson.

◐ TAs can act as a 'safe passage' between student and subject teacher.

◐ TAs are most effective in a lesson when they have a working knowledge of what's going to happen in it.

◐ TAs need to know when to intervene and when to leave the student to get on.

The most interesting aspect of the research projects was the part that looked at the TAs' perceptions of themselves. They recognise that they often have a perspective on a student that no one else on the staff has. They probably see that student more often and in a greater variety of situations than anyone else. That is a position of strength which can be used to develop a positive relationship with a youngster. This relationship can only work on the basis of mutual respect and the more astute TAs know that respect has to be earned.

They think that one of the foremost ways of earning respect is to be prepared to invest time in the relationship. In that time the TA would:

◐ listen;

◐ accentuate the positive;

◐ talk about school, concentrating on strengths and interests, hobbies, family and problems;

◐ share jokes;

◐ provide practical support, maybe buying ingredients for cooking when the students and their families have 'forgotten';

◐ forgive, but not forget (not holding grudges);

◐ explain the boundaries – what they will or won't accept, and why – and then stick to them.

TAs see lessons from the students' point of view. They see the shape of a lesson and how a pattern emerges. Lessons will start with the teacher talking for what seems an eternity, before setting a piece of writing. In this scenario, the TA contributes by sitting at the back and making some notes about the introduction. Once the students begin their writing, TAs fly around the classroom, reinforcing or reinterpreting for anyone who hasn't understood initially. (It should be noted, however, that the Key Stage 3 National Literacy Strategy has tried to point teachers in a slightly different direction: being more interactive, with more, short tasks set during the lesson.)

During this phase, TAs see themselves as a link between the students and the teacher. If they can't provide the information the student needs themselves (What did he say the hot stuff that comes out of the volcano is called? What colour do I use here? What's the date? What have I got to do?), they will approach the teacher to get the answer. This is generally because the students are too scared of the teacher to ask for themselves.

This is exhausting, if not exactly intellectually stimulating work. Repeating 'He said underline the title' 15 times is no one's idea of fun. It is not necessarily easy to reach this level of acceptance in the classroom. Picture the scene. It's a Year 9 English lesson. In walks Richard with Mrs Denny several paces behind. He is desperately trying to look cool and slumps into his desk. Mrs Denny, his TA, pulls up a chair and sits next to him. He turns away and tries to talk to his mate. Mrs D tells him to sit up straight and listen to the teacher. After that he simply ignores her. Richard doesn't want the stigma of being so stupid he needs a helper. It's especially embarrassing when everyone else in the class is messing about, and Mrs D tries to make him work.

TAs realise that this is a problem that will not go away of its own volition. Mrs D should simply look around for someone else who does want some help and work with them for a while. Then someone else will ask her a question. Before long, Richard will realise he is the only one not getting extra help. Then he will actively demand his share of attention.

TAs are frustrated that this use of their time is unfocused and untargeted. It is a reactive role; they go to the student making the most noise or the one who has had their hand up the longest, regardless of how trivial the problem is.

'TAs are aware of the positive influence they can have on a student's behaviour and attainment'

The TAs are aware of the positive influence they can have on a student's behaviour and attainment. This influence comes from the relationship that the TAs are able to form. We've talked about ways in which they earn the respect of the student. This is the core of the relationship. Richard knows that Mrs Denny is on his side – not uncritically and not blindly, but on his side, none the less. These children usually have enough in their lives stacked against them. They need all the support they can get. They will often fulfil their side of the deal by working hard for the TA.

Managing TAs

What TAs most want and need is direction. That, clearly, is your job. You tell them where to go, with whom to work and what that work should be. They then deliver the provision you've programmed. There is no reason why that work should not be within the mainstream classroom. You need to ensure that the work has a focus and meets the targets outlined in the IEP. A job description along the lines of the one offered here may help in agreeing the scope of each TA's role and their specific duties.

You also have to set up a system that evaluates the support. How does anybody – parent, child, TA, teacher, or OFSTED inspector – know whether the support

Teaching assistant job description

Name: _____

Job title: _____

Total no. of hours employed per week: _____

No. of direct hours of student contact: _____

No. of hours preparation/meetings/administration per week: _____

Role (delete if not applicable)

    a) Supporting students with statements

    Names of students _____ No. of hours _____

    _____ _____

    _____ _____

    b) General teaching assistant

    Group supported _____

    Subject _____

    Teacher _____

    Room _____

The teaching assistant will:
- arrive at and leave lessons punctually;
- work under the direction of the subject teacher;
- keep records at the direction of the SENCo;
- target support at students nominated by the SENCo or the subject teacher.

Specific duties _____

_____

Signed: _____ Teaching assistant

    _____ Line manager

Date: _____

has been effective? That's not the TA's responsibility, it's yours. You are the one who will have to justify what the TA does. Justification is easy if the TA is following an individual literacy programme, for example. If it's a child with a statement, the statement will provide literacy targets. The targets might involve learning National Literacy Strategy Framework sight words. You might deploy the TA for daily work on a reading recovery programme. Twice a year you can review the targets. Does Richard know all the Year 4 medium frequency words? Yes? His next target is the Year 5 words. All you need to do is to set up the programme that the TA delivers.

Monitoring and evaluating in-class support is a whole different ball game. Face it; there is no chance of Richard learning the NLS medium frequency Year 4 words in a geography lesson. If the statement, which is where the provision originates, says Richard needs a structured literacy programme, you'd better be doing that somewhere. If you're using the five hours of provision to help him to remember to underline the title and copy the notes on photosynthesis from the board in science, then the structured literacy programme will have to be covered in some other way. But if you have got it covered and you're going for in-class support, the only way forward is through the use of a contract.

Now I know what you're thinking. More paper. More time. It's a lot easier to send Mrs Denny along to design and technology with the instruction to help Richard get on. Mrs Ian, the D and T teacher, will be pleased to get an extra pair of hands. Richard needs the help. Mrs D will do as she's told. Everyone is happy. But what if Mrs Ian doesn't want an extra pair of hands, especially if Mrs D doesn't actually know anything about D and T? I spoke to one head of D and T who complained bitterly about the TA support in the lesson: 'It's like the blind leading the blind.'

There is still more to be managed if you're sending your TAs into the vicious world of subject departments. You will need to know what departments expect on a day-to-day basis from the TA. Subject staff will welcome help on a practical, though not menial, level. Mrs D would not be expected to hand out textbooks or do the photocopying, unless these are tasks that everyone takes turns to do. Rather, the TA should help students with the task in hand. Subject staff value TAs who are proactive and use their initiative. They like TAs who use their time flexibly. This might involve supporting a weak student, so that the teacher can work more freely and see more students. Alternatively, the TA will keep an eye on the many, while the teacher works with the few.

Subject teachers don't like it when the TA sits exclusively with one pupil. (If the TA is there as statement provision, the teacher will need to be aware of that and be made to understand the implications.) Nor do they like it when they get used to having a TA around and then the TA starts to miss lessons because you've asked them to carry out some administrative task or other. It may be that Mrs Denny needs to spend some time preparing for Richard's review, for example. You know it's important. Mrs Denny knows it's important. The subject teacher probably doesn't. Therefore, it's your responsibility to explain and avoid tension and ill feeling.

One of the recommendations in the DfES induction training for TAs is that they are based with departments, rather than following individual students. This can be done with TAs employed from the school's budget or from the LEA delegated budget. It is a system that is beginning to take off. It does have both strengths and weaknesses.

Strengths

It allows TAs to:

- build up subject knowledge, leading to being more secure and efficient;
- build more positive relationships with teachers;
- have access to departmental planning;
- attend and contribute to departmental meetings.

Weaknesses

It means that TAs:

- spend less time with one student;
- lose their cross-curricular picture of a student;
- have less contact with other TAs;
- lose skills in other departmental areas;
- lose contact with staff in other departments.

However you deploy them, TAs don't want to be thrown into situations without preparation. They value an induction programme that involves some input from you, but also involves peer support. They like to be paired with an experienced TA and shadow them for a period of time, in order to gain first-hand experience through the eyes of someone who has been there and done it. They also like to feel part of a team. They know that each of them has strengths that they contribute to the team. Your job is to exploit that, to build on it to the benefit of all.

Independence day

There's generally an initial murmur of disapproval when I suggest to TAs that their aim should be to make themselves redundant. What we, as educators, want is for pupils to become independent learners. We need to teach students skills that they can employ to solve problems for themselves. Too often, TAs oversupport their students, encouraging dependence rather than independence. However, the TAs relax when they realise that for 'their' student, independence day is a long way off. The student's skills may develop, but the demands of the curriculum will increase, which means that they may never catch up. If that is the situation, they will always need the support that TAs provide. That tends to make the TAs feel better. At their level of pay, the word 'redundant' has to be used very carefully.

"You got a B+ but you spelled photosynthesis wrong again!"

Nevertheless, there is a real danger that the TA will do too much, that Richard will be able to sit back and let Mrs D get on with the task for him. It is your responsibility to ensure that the TAs know when to leave the student to get on with the job and move away to help someone else.

You could set up role-playing scenarios of situations that they will come across in class:

- What should they do if a student has to copy down a board full of the subject teacher's writing?
- What should they do when the student says, 'I don't know how to start'?
- What should they do when the student has forgotten to bring a pen, again?

There will not be a single solution that fits each problem for every student, but this approach should generate a range of strategies that the TA can employ.

Chapter 6
The cavalry

Being a SENCo may be a lonely responsibility. Remember that you are not the only one feeling that way or with your particular problems. There's always someone around to offer support. In earlier chapters, we saw how the work of the SENCo is supported within the school. But sometimes the knowledge and expertise you need lies outside the school. We now look briefly at external sources of help and support.

SENCo Forum

You may be lucky enough to work in a local authority where there is an SEN network set up for you. The network might give you the opportunity to go to regular meetings with other secondary SENCos where representatives from the LEA attend to get your feedback or to answer your questions about policy and issues. The network might even be run for you by a friendly neighbourhood support service.

Sadly, not everyone has that level of support at hand. If you don't (or even if you do), you should subscribe to SENCo Forum, an online newsgroup. You may have discovered it already; a great many SENCos have, along with teachers, teaching assistants, LEA support staff, experts of all shapes and sizes and even the odd educational psychologist. Collectively, they add up to an essential resource.

Imagine you have a problem. Perhaps you have a question about dyscalculia. You need advice, information and support. You send an email to SENCo Forum; within 24 hours you have an e-sack full of replies. I must be honest and say that not all these replies will be particularly useful. Someone may complain about your use of apostrophes, someone else may complain that your problem was discussed thoroughly a month ago and another person will reply with a joke or ask your opinion about a recipe. However, in the midst of all this nonsense, a significant number of people will recognise your problem and have some similar experience or even a solution about which they are prepared to tell you. And they won't even try to charge you!

The biggest issue, with which many SENCos have to come terms, is the isolation of the post. Yes, you may have an army of TAs, but you probably won't be spoiled for choice when it comes to sharing a good whinge. No one else in the school will have the slightest idea what you are talking about. Even if they do, you won't get any sympathy or understanding. The only people in a position to empathise are other SENCos, or those that work alongside SENCos. This is the constituency of SENCo Forum. It's even recommended in the Code of Practice. (But don't let that put you off.)

To join SENCo Forum, send an email to majordomo@nfgl.gov. Leave the subject section blank, then in the main body of the email, write 'subscribe SENCo-forum'. And that's it. You'll receive a welcome message giving details of how to participate, how to access archives and how to leave.

Websites

While you are online, here a few suggestions for useful places to visit.

Recommended websites

Teacher Training Agency:
www.canteach.gov.uk/community/sen/index.htm
Pages include:

○ the national SEN specialist standards;

○ identifying your training needs;

○ SEN and the national standards;

○ using the national standards for SENCos;

○ ICT needs identification for complex/severe SEN;

○ SEN mandatory qualifications.

DfES SEN site: www.dfes.gov.uk/sen/senhomehtm

Becta Inclusion site: **www.becta.org.uk/inclusion**
A world of resources for teaching pupils with SEN.

Advisory Centre for Education: **www.ace-ed.org.uk**
A useful and informative guide to SEN designed for parents.

NASEN: **www.nasen.org.uk**
NASEN's aim is to promote the education, training, advancement and development of all those with SEN. They publish resources and journals, including *Support for Learning*, and organise courses and conferences on matters relating to SEN.

SEN resources for science: **www.issen.org.uk**
A NASEN-sponsored site.

General SEN resources:
www.geocities.com/SEN_resources
Useful definitions of SEN terms, and a host of downloadable resources.

The Literacy Trust:
www.literacytrust.org.uk/database.senissues
The Literacy Trust take on SEN.

Special Needs in Scotland:
www.ngflscotland.gov.uk/parentzone/pzsen

"So GOOD OF YOU TO COME AND SEE US AGAIN SO SOON, MR JONES!"

External agencies

As a member of an external agency, I have to make a heartfelt plea. You may have invited someone in to meet a student or a member of staff, or perhaps someone comes in on a weekly basis to teach a student. On the day, please check that the person in question is present. If not, phone and cancel the appointment. Otherwise you are sending the message that the service's time is unimportant and that it doesn't matter if someone struggles out to your school, only to find that the student is ill or on holiday or visiting a farm. It doesn't take much to organise a list of appointments in a daily diary and then for someone to cross-check against the school diary and the register.

Whatever systems or structures are in place in your LEA, what you get from your support services and external agencies depends entirely on the relationships you forge with the people who represent those services. If you can offer a bacon sandwich, or the vegetarian equivalent, to your educational psychologist and listen to them kindly as they talk about how nobody understands them, you'll have a greatly improved chance of a sympathetic response to your next request.

Anyway, here's a quick guide to some of the agencies you will come across.

The educational psychology service

Probably no group of people inspires such mixed emotions amongst SENCos as this one. They are beings of almost unimaginable power. However, it is always considerably easier to get an educational psychologist (EP) to say what they won't do rather than what they will do. They won't write reports for exam boards, unless you do all the testing for them. They won't work with individual students, especially the ones who could be saved by having a little time invested in them. They won't talk to geography teachers about strategies they could use with the students with problems in their class. Although this type of pre-emptive, early-intervention work is what the DfES would like from EPs, the majority of their time is at present taken up with statutory assessments.

However, you'll know when you need an EP. When everyone else has thrown up their hands in disgust and told you there's nothing that can be done for a child, that's when you need an EP. You want them to meet the student and then use their professional expertise and experience to suggest properly researched and proven strategies that stand a chance of being some use.

Sensory impairment support teams

These are staffed by nice people with experience and qualifications of a highly technical nature. They'll do all sorts of useful things for you and your students. They will enlarge worksheets, mend hearing aids, replace batteries, give support in lessons and write reports that are filled with so much specialist jargon that you can interpret them any way you like and no one will be any the wiser. Bless 'em and keep 'em, I say.

Behaviour support teams

Students with behavioural difficulties are the reason most teachers are leaving the profession, thinking of leaving the profession or applying for jobs in behaviour support teams. Forget the paperwork, the long hours and the inadequate pay. If classrooms were full of motivated, polite children who knew when to share a joke and when to shut up and get on, people would be clamouring to become teachers. I'm sure places like that exist, but we can't get jobs in them.

This is why, for once, the tabloid press, parents and teachers are united in being frightened to death by inclusion. No one worries about the hearing impaired student; you can rely on the hearing impairment service for support or just shout louder. The student who might hit you or anyone forced to sit next to them, or who will wang a chair at anyone who gets in their way – that's the one who gives inclusion a bad name. I sympathise, I really do. Often a youngster like this has been affected by a dreadful series of events or circumstances. It isn't their fault. But they take up so much time and so much emotional energy. We need help in helping them. That's the job of the behaviour support team or the educational psychology service. But when do you call in the behaviour support team? What do you expect them to do? What will they offer?

There is a tough decision to be made at the outset of this process. When do you put a student with behavioural difficulties on the SEN register, and when do you go down the route of pastoral intervention? The Disability Act now says that you can't discriminate against someone on the basis of special need. Therefore if you've placed someone on the SEN register because of their behavioural needs, the school cannot exclude them. Let's say Jerry has Tourette Syndrome. You put him on the register. Jerry goes on a geography field trip interviewing people. Jerry swears at a lady outside Marks & Spencer, bringing shame and disgrace on the school. No exclusion. Neither could you have prevented Jerry from going on the trip in the first place. Both would be seen as discriminatory.

There will obviously be times when you should put students with a behavioural need on the register. However, I would include them only if their literacy and numeracy skills were significantly delayed. But then you have a double problem. You have to develop their basic skills and address their behaviour. If you can do both, you don't need outside support. If you can support basic skills but not behaviour, you call on behaviour support. If it's the other way round, you might need help from a learning support service (see below). If you can cope in neither area, then you need the educational psychology service.

Having got the behaviour support team involved, what should you expect? At School Action Plus you should get an individual assessment of the student's needs, help with the IEP and regular monitoring, based on the reviews that you undertake. If the student is in receipt of a statement, you should expect individual support for them on a regular basis, weekly if needed. They should have one-to-one help in meeting the targets set in their IEP.

The learning support service

Students struggle with learning to read for a number of different reasons. Some have needs that can best be described as severe and complex. Perhaps someone else will have the experience, knowledge and resources that you lack. Perhaps they will just have more time – time to find the blockage and time to spend unblocking it. This where your LEA learning support service (LSS) can help.

They will support you at School Action Plus and when a student is in receipt of a statement. Exactly what they'll do varies depending on the LEA. You ought to be able to expect, at SA+, a detailed assessment, support with the resulting IEP and monitoring through attending reviews. For students with statements, they may offer one-to-one teaching; advice on materials, programmes and strategies; and regular visits so that you have someone to bounce ideas off.

The LSS tend to spend most of their time in school, working alongside teachers, students and TAs. They offer someone for you to talk to. They may have been doing the same thing at your neighbouring schools. If so, you can find out from the LSS what's happening there.

Afterword

So, can you survive and succeed as a secondary SENCo? Of course you can't. If you want to succeed, you will need to put in the sort of hours that would make Bob Cratchitt shudder. And that's OK if you're not worried about your family, your social life or your football team — all of whom will swiftly abandon you to an early grave. Alternatively, you could delegate everything to everybody, sit back, munch those cakes and watch life go by. And that's OK except you might fool OFSTED, but you won't fool the rest of the staff. They will be plotting against you within days.

The answer lies, inevitably, somewhere between the two extremes. There is simply too much to do for you to do it all properly. You need to identify priorities. They lie somewhere between your conscience, the Code of Practice, the rest of the staff, the LEA, and the students and their parents. And of course there is your life outside school. I would recommend you have one. It can be fun.

This book has tried to help you navigate your way towards your priorities. What matter most are the results the children achieve as a result of what you've put in place for them. If, like Bill, you can wave a piece of paper that shows that all your students are functional readers by the end of Year 9, you are fireproof. You can stand in front of OFSTED inspectors and tell them that what you do works. Just don't forget to be humble; you won't have done it alone.

I haven't spelt out an approach to inclusion, because that's out of our hands. Someone else will decide which students end up in our departments. Our job is to do the best we can with all of them. But if I had to say what inclusion really means, nobody put it better than the great American philosopher and educationalist Bruce Springsteen: 'Remember, in the end, nobody wins, unless everybody wins.'

Appendix 1

SEN English project

The strange case of Dr Jekyll and Mr Hyde

Assignment 1
News article

1 Read the section called 'The Carew Murder Case'. This sort of event would feature in a newspaper article of the day. Prepare a front page for *The London Herald*, 10 October 1885.

    a) First, look at the maid's story. Imagine you are the maid and write 50 words about what you saw. Begin like this: 'It was the most horrible thing I ever saw!'

    b) The maid identified Mr Hyde, so a newspaper reporter would go to interview people who have met him. Now, imagine you are Mr Enfield being interviewed. Begin like this: 'I never saw a man I so disliked.' Aim to write 50 words.

    c) Next the reporter visits Mr Utterson, who has set out deliberately to find out about Hyde. Imagine you are Mr Utterson being interviewed. Begin like this: 'The man hardly seemed human to me.'

Check the spelling and punctuation of your three interviews.

2 Begin to put your article together. Start with a headline that includes the name of Mr Hyde or Sir Danvers Carew. Also include a pun or some alliteration.

Think about the structure of your article.

    a) In your lead paragraph, grab the reader's attention. Include a few horrific details of the crime.

    b) Say where the crime happened (a house, near the river Thames).

    c) Say when the crime occurred.

    d) Say who was involved (include the MP and Mr Hyde).

    e) Now put in your three interviews.

    f) Talk about the public mood – horror, shock, distress – and about the need to catch and destroy the monster. The newspaper might make some guesses about who Hyde is and why he acted as he did (we do not know Carew was robbed).

    g) Produce some illustration for your article, e.g. Carew's purse and watch, or a map.

    h) Add some paragraph subheadings or pick out some key words using capitals.

    i) Design some adverts for contemporary products.

    j) Work out the layout on a sheet of A3 paper.

    k) Present your article along with the illustrations and adverts.

Appendix 2

How was your day, dear?

Thursday, 28 March

Arrive at school

Begin by trying to fix one of the department's ten computers (all carefully selected on account of being cheap). Fail. That's two down.

Briefing

Mrs M wants to talk to me about the unsatisfactory union advice that she has received and I offer to be her 'friend' in an interview with the head.

Lesson 1

Today is offically my 'admin' day, which means that, officially, I teach only one lesson. I have the rest of the day to deal with all the other things I don't have time to do during the rest of the week. So, the first lesson being 'free', it's back to computers. Fail again. Manage against all the odds to enlist Ray, the technician, to take a look.

Lesson 2

Readmission meeting about Scott. All goes well until I leave Scott alone with another member of staff. On my return, I have to spend 15 minutes talking Scott down.

Lesson 3

I need 260 literacy test scores to be loaded on to the shared area of the network and distributed in hard copy to departments. There are two missing papers; Maggie and I search but we find only one.

Give up search for the missing paper to plan the assessments of 14 functionally illiterate Year 7 pupils, each to last about 45 minutes. I still have to devise appropriate support strategies to suggest to staff, write summary sheets and IEPs and contact parents to discuss statement implementation plans.

Some LEA paperwork arrives on my desk. This will need to be a priority because some of next year's SEN funding is dependent on paperwork being accurate and up to date. I have a look and quickly calculate that it will take me between 6 and 8 hours to complete.

Lesson 4

Sit down with my list of people I need to speak to. Start by calling Sue at the Pupil Referral Unit. She's not available, but I speak with one of her colleagues to negotiate support arrangements for Michael the week after next. The conversation has an underlying tension: the PRU want to reduce their support as soon as possible; I don't want to have to disrupt the support timetable by pulling someone out to support the PRU students.

I also need to speak at length with the heads of English and maths to discuss how my scheme for implementing the school's literacy and numeracy strategies can be incorporated into the subject curricula. I know I can develop the Library Project materials for the literacy strategy, at a cost of perhaps 8 to 10 hours of preparation time. When the scheme starts, I am committed to delivering or organising a minimum of 9 hours' teaching a week. This has to be fitted in alongside the 16 hours to which I am currently committed – and the need to be on both sites.

Then there are the two parents of Key Stage 3 children. I promised that we would review progress after two weeks of term and it is now the end of the third week.

And I must speak with all of Ben's teachers to try to head off what seems like a revolt against his inclusion in their classes. One teacher is refusing to have him in the class; others are muttering about allowing him in for the moment – but not next year. I need to write his IEP; his mother will be clamouring for it before long.

Appendix 2

Break

The bell goes and I set out for the staff room. After three or four minutes of herding students gently towards the designated areas, I get as far as the crossroads. I meet Mrs D and start to arrange a time for us to discuss the literacy strategy. Interrupted by the principal, scurrying hotfoot out of the coastal heads meeting. He regales us with the secondary school version of the early literacy strategy that he's just heard about and wants to know if we'd like to get involved. I think my plan is better. After 16 minutes I have almost made it to the foot of the stairs to the staffroom – but the bell rings.

Lesson 5

Scott is reluctant to attend his next lesson, so I have to persuade him gently to go.

I get the phone numbers of the parents who I might need to contact this weekend to arrange reviews.

Talk to Ray about the computers. He says they'll be easy to fix.

Scott turns up at Learning Support, saying that he doesn't know what lesson he's got. I suspect that he does, but look up his timetable anyway. It says IT, GPu, Room 24. We go along, but bless me, the timetable's wrong – it isn't his group! After a few more minutes of checking and searching, I give up. I tell Scott he can stay in Learning Support and do his maths work on the computer. (After umpteen years of wasting hours on hunting for students or lessons because the school timetable isn't right, I've decided I'm not going to spend time on it any longer.)

Gemma and her supporter turn up, explaining that she became very distressed during RE, so they felt it best to come out. I load a spelling programme for them to work on. I head for the staff room to try to sneak a coffee, but I'm met by Steven, who has been given permission by Mr M to leave his lesson (other kids giving Steven a hard time) to come and see me. Mr M has no idea whether anyone is in Learning Support or whether I'm teaching statemented pupils in there, but he has sent Steven anyway. I send Steven to Tutorial Support, trying to explain gently that I see his problem, but I'm really not the one to sort it.

Next I meet Sean, who tells me that his art teacher has given him the option of staying in the lesson or coming out (from which I gather that he's got himself into a strop). He has chosen to come out and he says the sheet that he's supposed to be copying from has print that is too small for him (nystagmus bad, eyes hurting). Much of the clear and specific advice that I spend many hours preparing and distributing is similarly ignored. I take Sean to reprographics and enlarge the material for him. Someone meets us and says that Sean is expected in Mr B's office for a meeting. I escort him there, but they're not ready for him, so I allow him to come with me to Learning Support.

On arrival back at Learning Support, we are met by Sean and Scott, and by Gemma with her helper. We are immediately joined by Kyle, breathing fire and tears in equal measure, having stormed out of English again. I have to talk to him in the office for a few minutes to calm him down.

I now have 8 minutes to set up the computers and resources for my lesson. As I pick up my bag and the computer on which I've been working, the phone rings. It's the office to say there is an 'urgent fax' coming through for me right now and would I like to come and collect it. It's from a London Social Services department asking for information about a student. They want information that includes assessment scores for Key Stages 1, 2 and 3; the SEN stage; and a copy of his latest IEP. And they want it all by last Thursday.

Lesson 6

I leave to teach a lesson that I haven't really prepared properly but which goes quite well, except for a spat with a testosterone-laden 15-year-old.

Lunch break

Mrs W wants to know whether I've completed the summary information for Colchester Institute about the students in the Alternative Curriculum group. Alison gives me the list of Ben's teachers with whom I need to speak, and the choices made by Learning Support staff about courses they'd like to attend. I need to talk these through with Debbie, find out how much training budget we've got, and write out an application for each, justifying participation against 'College and Departmental Development Plan targets'. As I leave, Mrs M. asks me to distribute copies of a news-sheet to union members.

I eat some of my lunch in the car. The rest is going to stay uneaten. Back at my office, Ray, the technician, tells me that Mr R wants to start all of the maths groups on ILS on Monday and wants them all enrolled in the Maths Concepts and Skills programme at level 3.5. Ray is not quite sure about how to execute this command so I will have to show him again. But I will also have to go and talk to Mr R because enrolling globally at this level means the least able students will find the work impossibly difficult, so they will not enjoy ILS or get much from it.

Just time to fit in a visit to Mr M to explain that, contrary to popular belief, I don't spend all of my time sitting on my backside in Learning Support and teachers really shouldn't send students to see me 'on spec'.

Lesson 7

The bell goes and my two statemented tutees have arrived. So has Ms L who says she urgently needs to discuss Kyle, who has become aggressive and difficult in his last three English lessons, eventually walking out or being sent to Learning Support. We agree that a change of key supporter in these lessons is probably necessary and I wonder how to make the arrangement without hurting any feelings. Steven has also returned.

I redirect Steven to Tutorial Support, explain the task to the statemented tutees, go into the library to show Ray the ILS routines – and find classroom-phobic Amy is still there on her own with no work. I talk to her and find her some work. Then spend 15 minutes with my tutees, before setting them a further task to do while I begin trawling the shared area for the Key Stage data and other information for the London Social Services department. Most of it is not there.

End of school

Bus duty. Then walk with Mrs K on her way out of school to discuss how her first full week with Gemma has gone. Return to office and speak with Miss T to praise her for her efforts to make a very difficult subject accessible to Gemma. Mrs M wants to talk to me about an incident in which some boys have urinated into the bin in the disabled toilet and to ask whether we need to have a key located in the office for use by designated pupils. I explain that Emily sometimes can't wait that long and that, anyway, it needs to be accessible for disabled visitors to the school.

Mr W has read his sheet about the role of the key worker and wants to take up the written advice and liaise with me about ensuring that procedures conform to LEA requirements. I'm now close to being late for my one session of weekly exercise. I'm told that the London borough has phoned again, asking whether someone can attend the case conference in London – on Monday. I work out that the boy has a sister also in care. We phone to ask whether they want information on her too. As I walk out of the door, the reply comes back, 'Er, yes, I suppose so.'

Head for home.

Resources

Literacy programmes

Corrective Reading. Englemann *et al.*, SRA McGraw-Hill

Reading Workshop. Ward Lock

THRASS. THRASS UK, www.thrass.com

Basic Reading for Secondary Students. Grant Von Harrison and
    John C Wilkinson, OTSU/GVH

DfES (2002) *Literacy Progress Units – Spelling*

Reading books

Penguin Series. Oxford, Ginn

Five Minute Thrillers. Wisbech, LDA

Ten Minute Thrillers. Wisbech, LDA

Spirals. Hampshire, Nelson Thornes

Headwork Readers. Oxford, Oxford University Press

Zoom series. Oxford, Ginn

Reference

Basic Skills Agency (2002) *It Doesn't Get Any Better*.

DfES Publications (2001) *Special Educational Needs Code of Practice*.

DfES Publications (2001) *SEN Toolkit*.

DfES Publications (2000) *National Curriculum 2000 Inclusion Statement*.

Joint Council for General Qualifications *Regulations and Guidance relating to Candidates with Particular Requirements*.

TTA (1998) *National Standards for Special Educational Needs Co-ordinators*.

TTA (1999) *National Special Educational Needs Specialist Standards*.

Software

IEP Writer. LearnHow Publications, www.learnhowpublications.co.uk

SuccessMaker. Pearson Education, www.successmaker.com

Wordshark 3. White Space Ltd, www.wordshark.co.uk